The Kindness of the Hangman

Even in Hell, There is Hope

*A young German boy's true story of tragedy and triumph,
from the depths of despair in Auschwitz and Buchenwald
to an extraordinary new life in America.*

By Henry Oster and Dexter Ford

Higgins Bay Press

Manhattan Beach, California

Library of Congress Cataloging-in-Publication Data

Oster, Henry, 1928-
Ford, Dexter, 1953-
The Kindness of the Hangman

To purchase The Kindness of The Hangman, and to learn more about Henry Oster,
his ongoing research into The Holocaust, and his upcoming speaking engagements and
public appearances, please visit www.TheKindnessOfTheHangman.com

ISBN: 978-0-578-14445-0

Published by Higgins Bay Press
2607 Maple Avenue
Manhattan Beach, California 90266
310 546 1781

dexter@dexterford.com

Introduction:

The creation of this book began in Dr. Henry Oster's Beverly Hills optometry office. I was one of his many patients, and an annoying one at that.

As he made glasses for me—pair after pair—I always found a way to complain about my prescription. If we had agreed that my right eye needed astigmatism correction at a certain angle, by the time the glasses were made, I would want a slightly different twist. Finally, in desperation, he gave me a pair of old trial frames—ancient, odd-looking adjustable glasses that would let me change the orientation of my lenses to my heart's content.

I started out a patient, but I quickly became a friend. I was curious about how everything worked, and Henry, a natural teacher, loved to explain it all. Appointments that would have lasted 10 minutes with another optometrist sometimes went on for hours, the two of us chattering away while his office staff tried to hold off his other patients.

I wound up showing up for his famous lunches downstairs at Nibblers Restaurant on Wilshire Boulevard, joining in while he held court with an ever-changing cast of friends and patients. Henry is 25 years older than I am, but I was fascinated by his energy and contagious joy at being alive. Henry seemed to treat each new day like an unexpected gift, and he was determined to enjoy it all and coax other people around him do the same. He was—and is—just a hell of a lot of fun to be with.

One day, while he was trying, with limited success, to fit me with yet another set of contact lenses, I noticed a faded, slightly crooked, blue-black tattoo on his left forearm. B7648.

"How did you get that, Henry?" I asked.

This is the story of how it got there. And how, against incomprehensible odds, after losing almost everything a human being can lose, Henry Oster survived to tell that story.

Dexter Ford
Manhattan Beach, California, July, 2014

Dedication:

The Kindness of the Hangman is dedicated to the memory
of my parents, Hans Isidor Oster and Elisabeth Haas Oster,
and to the memory of the 12 million innocent victims,
including 6 million Jews, 1.5 million children, and
16 members of my own family who died as a result
of German atrocity in World War II.

It is also dedicated to Ivar Segalowitz, my best friend
in this world from the day we banged elbows
on a wooden sleeping shelf in the Buchenwald concentration
camp in 1945 until his sad passing in 2014.
When we had nothing left to lose, we found each other.

Henry Oster
Woodland Hills, California
July 31, 2014

Chapter 1

A German boy.

A long time ago, I was a five-year-old German boy. Heinz Adolf Oster.

I was an inquisitive, energetic little wise guy with a shock of black hair, a double dose of curiosity and a limited ability to stand still for any length of time.

One of my earliest memories is of walking on the tree-lined sidewalks of Cologne, the majestic, historic German city that was my home, going out with my father to vote in the 1933 German national election. That was, of course, the election that allowed Adolf Hitler and his National Socialist Party—the Nazis—to seize power in Germany.

I had no idea of how important that day was, or what that election would lead to. Nobody did, probably not even Adolf Hitler himself. But I do remember my father—Hans Isidor Oster—taking my hand as we walked out of our apartment, and down the street to the voting booth. My father was tall, serious, thin, and respected. People on the street would recognize him, smile, tip their hats to him. Friends stooped down to see me, his little boy all dressed up like Little Lord Fauntleroy, on our adventure to the voting booth. I remember he smoked cigarettes constantly—it seemed to make him more grand, more mature, more important.

It was a rare treat, getting to go out with my Dad, just the two of us. He was the manager of several small department stores, and he was usually very busy, so as with most German children—and most children the world over at the time—I spent much more time with my mother than with my father.

I remember that after we left the polling place, he took me to a confectioner's shop to get *schlagsahne*—vanilla-flavored whipped cream— which was kind of like going out for ice cream today. I was very happy. It was a big day for me.

I was an only child. I lived with my mother and father in this cosmopolitan, elegant city in western Germany. Cologne is known for its ancient Gothic cathedral, the Dom, its twin towers of lace-work masonry thrusting what seemed like miles above the city.

We didn't worship in the Catholic Dom, but we were, first and foremost, a good German family. We had no reason to feel that were any less German than anybody else. My father was a veteran of the German Army, the Wehrmacht. He had fought in the Great War—World War I—just like millions of other German men. He had been wounded in the war: he had a scar on his cheek where a piece of shrapnel had hit him during

Photo: Henry Oster Archive

*Heinz (Henry) Oster, age 5,
with his father, Hans Isidor Oster,
in Cologne, Germany, 1933.*

an artillery barrage. He had been awarded a medal for bravery. He had no reason not to fight in the defense of his country, right or wrong—to fight for his Fatherland. Like any other good German.

The only thing that was different about us was that we were Jewish. Which, at the time, wasn't a big thing to me. The only way that I could sense any difference between myself and the other German kids I knew was that I went with my family to synagogue every Friday night, instead of going to church on Sunday. And I went to a German Jewish school, where we were taught Hebrew, along with all the other usual subjects. But I had no sense that we were different, no better or worse, than any other German family.

It was a comfortable, normal life. I was just a restless German kid, with a nice family, in a busy German city. But when Hitler and the Nazis came to power—just about the time I was old enough to have any idea of what was going on around me— everything started to go haywire.

The first time I began to feel that there was anything wrong—my first experience of being singled out, being different, being persecuted—was my first day of school, in 1934.

Like every other kid who ever went to school for the first time, I was frightened, a little apprehensive. I was six years old now, and I was going into the unknown world, away from my mother and father for the first time, ready or not.

My parents walked me to school: I was carrying, very seriously, a little leather backpack with a tiny blackboard, a piece of chalk on a string, and a sponge to use as an eraser. I was wearing knee pants, stockings and a little hat, like a beret, which identified me as a first-year student.

Like all the other children, I carried a huge cardboard cone that my parents had given me. It looked like a megaphone or a dunce cap, filled with all kinds of lovely things—candies and little toys.

It was a German tradition to send kids off to the their first day of school with this—we called it a *Zuckertüte*, or "sugar cone"—to help us feel more comfortable as we went into this strange new world. We weren't allowed to open them—they were tied with red cellophane at the top, to keep us from getting at the goodies inside—until we got home from school. It was a sort of reward, something to look forward to. Mine was almost as tall as I was, or at least that's the way it felt to me.

But when we came out of school that day, holding our precious sugar cones, we were smashed by a gang of young Hitler Youth, the *Deutsches Jungvolk* and *Jungmädel*. They were a big, noisy mob, waiting outside on the sidewalk, boys and girls a little older than we were. They were all very proud of themselves, all dressed up like little Nazi Boy Scouts and Girl Scouts.

We were scared to death. Some of my classmates were crying. We were little kids, just six years old. And now, after our first nervous day of school, we were being attacked by this screaming Nazi mob for no reason.

My parents—and all the other Jewish kids' parents—were waiting outside the school to pick us up and walk us home. But there was nothing they could do to help us. They had all been shoved out of the way by the Hitler Youth leaders, young toughs in their teens and twenties.

I remember looking up and seeing a sea of uniforms and angry faces. The people were yelling and taunting us, these furious kids with their Nazi neckerchiefs, all with the same swastika slides at their throats. The boys had daggers on their belts. They were just kids, 10 to 14 years old, but they each had their little Nazi knives.

In the background we could just see the brownshirt Nazi organizers, and the proud parents of the Hitler Youth, standing with their arms crossed. They were obviously enjoying this, watching their children showing the little Jewish kids just who's who and what's what.

The children threw rocks at us. They hit us with sticks. We were all forced to run this gauntlet to escape, to get through to our parents and safety.

The Hitler Youth paid special attention to attacking our *Zuckertüten*. They bashed at them with their sticks, trying to knock them out of our hands. And when one broke open, they all scrambled on the ground to steal our candies and toys.

Eventually, a couple of Cologne city policemen, who were not necessarily Nazis then, showed up and stopped the attack, giving me and the other Jewish kids enough time and space to make it through to our parents.

Photo: Henry Oster Archive

*Elisabeth Haas Oster and
Heinz (Henry) Oster, 1928*

Photo: Henry Oster Archive

*Heinz (Henry) Oster, age 6.
Cologne, Germany, 1934.*

None of us were seriously hurt—just some scrapes and small cuts, a little bit of blood here and there. But we were all shocked.

I had gone to school that morning, full of excitement and anticipation, anxious about how well I was going to do in the classroom.

When I finally made it home that afternoon, my world was a much darker, more dangerous place. My life would never be the same. The world would never be the same.

Illustration: Calvin College Archive

Nazi propaganda aimed at German children. An illustration from a 1936 anti-Jewish children's book published in Germany, "Trust no Fox on his Green Heath, And No Jew on his Oath", encouraging German children to ostracize Jewish children from schools. "Away with all the Jewish Breed" reads the text. The book was published by influential Nazi Julius Streicher, and was written by Elvira Bauer, an 18-year-old German art student.

Chapter 2

A Nation in Search Of A Leader.

As a six-year-old kid, I had no idea of what was going on politically, of course. But Germany was in a state of upheaval at the time. The country had lost World War I, and the countries that had won—France and England, predominantly—were exacting war reparations, taking away territory and huge amounts of money that Germany really didn't have.

Just as in America, it was a time of financial hardship, a great depression. In the 1920s and early 1930s there was huge unemployment. Thousands of ragged men roamed out on the streets, many of them shell-shocked and wounded war veterans, with nothing to do except complain and plot and scheme.

World War l had been a nightmare for its soldiers, no matter on which side they fought. Trench warfare was horrifying, with thousands dying to gain—or lose—a few yards of mud and barbed wire. Disease ran rampant through every army. Machine guns, artillery, tanks, poison gas and bombs from airplanes and Zeppelins killed millions. The survivors were, as are soldiers today, damaged forever. Millions were wounded physically. Nearly all were wounded in their hearts and their souls. Europe would never be the same again.

There was crazy inflation in the German economy: the same amount of money was worth less and less every day. A loaf of bread would cost a million marks—a whole wheelbarrow full of nearly worthless paper money.

When Hitler came to power, maneuvering behind the scenes after that 1933 election, the German people were willing to follow a leader— any leader—who could convince them that he had a way out, a way to make Germany strong and wealthy again.

He enlisted all those rootless, unemployed men, all those ex-soldiers and veterans, and gave them a structure in which to live. He gave them a cause. Now they had a gang to join, something to believe in, however bizarre and inhuman that cause turned out to be. He organized anybody who would listen to him. He let men out of the jails and converted them to the Nazi cause—hardened criminals, uneducated bums, low-life elements of society. He made them believe that they could be a part of something that could make Germany great again.

He blamed the Jews for nearly all of Germany's problems.

Dictators and other leaders often inflate their own status and power by convincing their people that they are under attack by some "other"— any group that looks, or acts, or believes differently.

It's happening now, in the Middle East. It's happening in Russia, and in Darfur. It happened in Bosnia, in the 1980s. It's happening in North Korea and in Syria. It happened in Rwanda, when millions of people were hacked to death by their neighbors, incited by their leaders.

To see it in action, just listen to the right-wing pundits on American television. "Everything would be great", they always seem to say. "If it wasn't for 'them'". 'Them" can be anyone. Blacks. Jews. Latinos. The Irish. The Italians. Muslims. Immigrants. People who go to college. People who don't go to college. Elitists. Welfare recipients. Gays. Union workers. Even women. Anybody who is not "us".

Herman Goering, a member of the Nazi hierarchy and the commander of the German Air Force, the *Luftwaffe*, said it himself during his 1946 war-criminal trial at Nuremberg:

"…the people can always be brought to the bidding of the leaders. That is easy. All you have to do is tell them they are being attacked and denounce the pacifists for lack of patriotism and exposing the country to danger. It works the same way in any country."

Feelings of suspicion and hatred of Jews had been lingering for centuries—and it was still going strong at the beginning of the 20th century.

Like many people around the world, including even hero pilot Charles Lindbergh and American industrialist Henry Ford, Hitler believed that Jews had formed an international conspiracy. Allied with the Communists who had come to power in Russia, they were, he fantasized, plotting to dominate the world's political and financial institutions and, eventually, the world itself. He also believed that some Jews, allied with Communists, had caused Germany to lose World War I by fomenting labor strikes, political subversion and revolution behind the lines—a myth known as *Dolchstoßlegende*: the Stab In The Back.

This myth was promulgated by German politicians in the period immediately after the first war to deflect blame for Germany's defeat. In 1918 Germany's allies were quickly surrendering, and its army was running out of money, supplies and reserves, facing the ever-stronger forces of France, the British Empire, Belgium and the United States. Its defeat was inevitable. But the Stab In The Back theory allowed many Germans—one of them Hitler himself, then an injured and blinded corporal in the German Army—to believe that Germany had not really been defeated, but that its war effort had been undermined from within. By "others". By Jews and Communists.

Like many nationalists the world over, Hitler believed that the people of his home countries—in his case Austria and Germany——were the greatest in the world.

It's a common belief. Not too reasonable, but common. "I am pretty great.", the logic goes. "Everybody who is like me also seems great.

"In fact, the more they are like me, the greater they seem to be. Now that I think about it, everybody who is not like me seems less great. How to explain this? They must be inferior."

Hitler was forming his ideology at a time when Eugenics—the pseudo-science that supposed that almost all human behavior was genetically inspired—was gaining popularity with white academics and leaders around the globe. In many countries, including Britain and the United States, the Eugenics movement advanced the idea that it was the right and responsibility of governments to prevent the "unfit"—pretty much anybody who didn't look or act like the people in power—from reproducing.

Society could be "purified" by preventing, by force if necessary, the "unfit" from having children, who if allowed to live would supposedly be "unfit" as well. Hitler wasn't the only person in the world who had toyed with the idea that in order to prevent "inferior" people from polluting any particular society, it might be a great idea to prevent them from having children. Or worse.

This wasn't just a fringe idea, held by a few outlying nutcases. It was the law of the land of the United States of America. In a chilling 1927 Supreme Court Decision, *Buck v. Bell*, the court upheld a Virginia law that allowed sterilizing, against their will, people held in state mental institutions who were judged "feebleminded"—a term that could mean just about anything.

Carrie Buck, an adopted 17-year-old girl, was raped by her foster mother's nephew and had become pregnant. To avoid the shame of having a pregnant, unmarried daughter around the house, her adoptive family had her committed to a state mental institution.

Carrie Buck's biological mother, Emma Buck, was a poor woman who, after her husband deserted the family, was accused of immorality and prostitution and was committed to the Virginia State Colony for Epileptics and Feebleminded. Carrie was judged by the Commonwealth of Virginia to be "feeble-minded" and "promiscuous" when she became pregnant. With no credible evidence—she was, in reality, nothing more sinister than a confused teenaged rape victim. Her baby daughter, Vivian, was also judged "feebleminded" at the age of 7 months, after a cursory visit by a Red Cross social worker, because on the day of the visit Vivian didn't appear to be as active or alert as another baby girl her age lying next to her.

The 8-to-1 majority decision was written by Justice Oliver Wendell Holmes, Jr., one of the most respected judges in American history. It reads like something right out of Adolf Hitler's Nazi manifesto, *Mein Kampf*. Which, in fact, was partly inspired by the American Eugenics movement.

Justice Holmes wrote:

"We have seen more than once that the public welfare may call upon the best citizens for their lives. It would be strange if it could not call upon those who already sap the strength of the state for these lesser sacrifices. . . . It is better for all the world, if instead of waiting to execute degenerate offspring for crime, or to let them starve for their imbecility, society can prevent those who are manifestly unfit from continuing their kind. The principle that sustains compulsory vaccination is broad enough to cover cutting the Fallopian tubes. Three generations of imbeciles are enough."

Justice Holmes' decision refers to the "three generations of imbeciles", meaning Emma Buck, Carrie Buck and Carrie's newborn daughter Vivian.

As a result of this Supreme Court decision, Carrie Buck, as well as her sister Doris, were sterilized against their will. Doris was lied to, and was sterilized secretly during an appendectomy. At least 60,000 other Americans would suffer the same fate under similar laws, some 20,000 in the State of California alone. These laws would later become the model for Nazi Germany's similar *Erbgesundheitsrecht* laws, under which 375,000 people, including many who were merely deaf or blind, were sterilized by the Nazi state.

In Germany, it wasn't long before being a Gypsy, or a homosexual—or, in my particular case, a Jew—were also considered evidence of being "unfit" to be a German. And the methods used to "cleanse" German society of us "unfit" people—even though most German Jews were successful, well-educated and, in the case of my father, a war hero—quickly escalated.

From 1933 to 1939, the Nazis moved from sterilization to actually murdering the "unfit" by the hundreds of thousands. During this time, American Eugenics leaders were encouraging—and even financially supporting—the German Eugenics movement.

All the way up until 1939, the Rockefeller Foundation—to this day, one of the premier American philanthropic organizations—supported Nazi-inspired studies on racial "superiority" at the Kaiser Wilhelm Institute of Anthropology, Human Heredity, and Eugenics, even after it was obvious that this pseudo-science was being used to legitimize the persecution of Jews and other vulnerable segments of Germany society. One of the scientists whose studies were funded by the Rockefeller Foundation was Doctor Josef Mengele, whose bizarre experiments and role in selecting gas-chamber victims in Auschwitz later earned him the title "Angel of Death".

Long before the first Jews were killed in concentration camps, Nazi Germany's *Aktion T4* program, which ran from 1939 to 1941, ordered German and Austrian doctors to murder 70,273 physically or mentally handicapped people by lethal medication, starvation or poison gas. The program continued unofficially throughout the war, with a total of over 200,000 deaths by 1945.

What became of Carrie Buck, the 17-year-old rape victim who, along with her mother and daughter, had been labeled so "feebleminded" that they should not be allowed to reproduce and pollute society? When Carrie and her sister Doris were interviewed by a journalist 56 years later, it was obvious that both were intellectually normal. At the age of 77, Carrie read newspapers every day and worked on crossword puzzles to pass the time.

And what of Carrie's little daughter Vivian, whose birth had so enraged the Commonwealth of Virginia, as well as eight justices of the U.S. Supreme Court? In her second year of school, at the age of seven, she was listed on the honor roll. As did many children in that age before antibiotics, she died of a digestive disease the next year.

Using the Eugenics laws of the United States of America as an

Photo: U.S. Holocaust Memorial Museum Archive

Hitler Youth Rally, Berlin, Germany, 1933

inspiration, Adolf Hitler truly believed that all other nations, and all other races, were inferior to his. He was especially afraid of Communism and he believed, without any actual evidence, that Jews were the biological foundation of Communism—that Communism was as much a product of inferior genetics as of a political movement.

While a few of the original leading Soviet Communists had been Jews—no big surprise, considering the previous Russian Czarist government's own virulent anti-Semitism—Josef Stalin, Hitler's equally cruel counterpart leading the Soviet Union, had purged them from the Communist Party ranks well before Hitler came to power in the 1930s.

Hitler's biggest fear—that of a Jewish/Communist conspiracy to dominate Europe, and eventually the world—never existed. His main thrust in World War ll—and the misguided effort that brought down his "Thousand-Year Reich"—would be his suicidal assault on the Soviet Union. An effort propelled, with essentially no basis in reality, by his unreasoning hatred for Jews—Jews who were not guilty of the crimes of which he and his National Socialist cronies had accused them.

Within a month of his taking power in 1933, Hitler had already established Dachau, the first concentration camp, on the outskirts of Munich, the home of the Nazi revolution, to imprison anybody who had the courage to oppose him.

In order to build a strong, seemingly invincible Germany, he knew he had to start with the youngest members of society. So he organized the Hitler Youth, and other social clubs, to indoctrinate every non-Jewish German kid into his crazy—but far from uncommon—view of the world.

By the time those kids grew up, from 1933 to 1939, he had built an entire country that was dedicated to what they had been taught. A country that would follow him, unquestioning. A country that could do amazing things, that could dominate an entire continent. And which could do unspeakable, horrible things. Things we can hardly imagine could have ever happened, things that most of us believe human beings, let alone "civilized" human beings, are not capable of doing.

It was not conceivable then. It is not conceivable now. It can't happen. It couldn't happen.

But it did. I was there. It happened to my neighbors, and my relatives. It happened to my family. It happened to me.

Haas family outing, Cologne, Germany, circa 1924. Elisabeth Haas,
Henry Oster's mother, is seated in the middle, holding the oar.

Chapter 3

Jews in Germany.

Historians tell us that the first Jews who settled in Germany were probably emigrants from Rome. The first documented Jewish community in Germany dates back to 321 AD, in the city of Cologne.

Which happens to be my home town. So when Adolf Hitler (who was not born in Germany, but in Austria) and his Nazi friends decided that Jews like me, my mother and my father were unfit to live in "his" Germany, we had already been living there for over 1600 years.

Antagonism against Jews in Europe had been common for many centuries. The term "ghetto" was originally an Italian word, an abbreviation of "borghetto", or "little village". Ghettos were the walled-off parts of cities where Jews were forced to live, apart from Christians and other groups, first in Venice and Rome and then in other Roman cities.

Waves of persecution—called pogroms—went on, off and on, for hundreds of years. Sometimes Jews were attacked, segregated, and vilified. Sometimes the pendulum went the other way, and we were more accepted into European society.

Jews had been persecuted as convenient scapegoats, in Europe and elsewhere, for nearly a thousand years. In the time of the First Crusade, starting in 1096, Christians in Germany were encouraged to attack and exterminate any non-believers. Entire German Jewish communities were massacred. Muslims, who were no more popular than Jews, were a long way away, in the Holy Land. But we Jews were right there in town, ready to be slaughtered.

During the Black Plague of the 14th century, the rat-born disease that killed as many of half the inhabitants of many major cities of central Europe, Jews were blamed, scapegoated and even massacred, even though they had nothing to do with the disease or the deaths.

Rumors spread that the cause of the plague was Jews poisoning the wells of Christians, inciting the panicked populace to react against Jewish communities in horrible ways.

Because Jews were often isolated in ghettos in the cities, limiting the spread of the plague, and because Jews at that time practiced generally higher standards of hygiene than other cultures, the Jewish communities often suffered far fewer instances of the disease. This caused suspicion among the Catholics and other inhabitants, who responded, in many cases, by massacring Jewish communities, often burning entire populations of Jews, along with their houses and synagogues.

In 1349, the Jewish population of Cologne was exterminated. Men, women and children were beaten, beheaded and burned alive, their homes stolen, their possessions looted. And by 1351, just two years later, as many as 60 major German Jewish communities, as well as 150 smaller villages, had been destroyed.

In some cases communities of Jews chose to burn their own houses, with their families still inside, to prevent the mobs from dragging them out and burning or lynching them.

Charles IV, the Holy Roman Emperor, decreed that the property of Jews was forfeit as a result of these atrocities, giving the local authorities even less incentive to prevent the wholesale destruction of the Jewish people.

Jesus of Nazareth, after all, was a Jew who was persecuted and murdered by the Romans.

Finally, in the 1860s, German Jews—and Germans of other non-Christian religions—were given full rights under German law. After nearly 1500 years of separation and repression, when the North German Confederation was established in 1869, Jews were allowed all the privileges due any other German citizen.

We could go to German public schools and universities. We could become lawyers, and eventually even judges. And due in part to an odd tenet of Christianity, Jews had long been successful in what became, over the centuries, the banking industry.

Like present-day Muslims, early Christians had been prevented by their own religious leaders and beliefs from charging interest when lending money to other Christians.

Jews, on the other hand, were free to lend money to Christians, and as such were both sought after, when Christians and Christian leaders needed to borrow money, and reviled because the ability to lend money and collect interest made some Jews wealthier than their Christian neighbors.

Because of our belief in learning and education, Jews tended to succeed in German society, and become visible as leaders in business, in law, and the other professions. And to some more-backward parts of German society, this reignited jealousy, bigotry and resentment against the Jews.

Some businesses had become huge conglomerates which were legitimately dominated by Jews: banking, the motion picture industry, science, medicine and, the most important area, the law. By the 1930s a huge number of German judges were Jewish.

As a visible, historically persecuted minority in Germany—there were about 600,000 Jews in a country of 60 million Germans, just 1% of the population—Jews thought that one way to become accepted, to become more tolerated, was to blend in, become assimilated, and make a contribution to the society we lived in.

Once we were given the freedom to attend universities, we did that by educating ourselves, by working hard, by becoming, in many ways, more German and less Jewish. But by succeeding in all these important fields in the society, we became disproportionately visible.

From the 1860s all the way to the 1930s, most German Jews became highly integrated into German life. Like me, almost all spoke German as a first language, rather than the Yiddish of many other Jewish communities in Eastern Europe. Many Jews were not religious at all. And Jews played a vital role in German society, and even the German military. In World War l, a greater percentage of German Jews fought for their country than any other political, religious or ethnic group in the nation.

12,000 German Jewish soldiers died during that war, and my father, among many others, was wounded and decorated for heroism.

The German officer who awarded Corporal Adolf Hitler the Iron Cross, First Class, during World War I was Lieutenant Hugo Gutmann. Who just happened to be Jewish.

Chapter 4

The Rise of the Nazis.

In 1934 I was only six, but I knew that we were a pretty well-to-do family. How did I know this? Well, unlike many of the other families we knew, we had a radio. We felt very lucky, very modern, very avant-garde.

I remember sitting on my mother's knee and listening, in the dark, to the broadcast of the funeral of President Von Hindenburg. The occasion was sad and solemn, and the music, over the scratchy radio, was as heavy as a lead blanket.

Hitler had already moved to take over the government the year earlier, after the 1933 elections. But when Hindenburg, who was a very old and tired man, finally passed away the next year, Hitler was free to consolidate his power and declare himself "Fuhrer and Reichskansler", the unchallenged head of state.

Hitler wasted no time in turning Germany into a flag-covered, swastika-emblazoned, Jew-hating police state.

Because we had a radio, we could listen to many of Hitler's speeches. And being a good German boy who knew nothing of what was beginning to unfold, I was mesmerized. Like him or not, he was an amazing speaker. I remember being thrilled by his voice screaming out of the radio, and hearing the crowd in the background roaring "Heil" at his command.

We could see their fervor spreading all over our city like a tide of blood. "*Heil Hitler*" (Hail Hitler) became the common greeting, both coming and going. The Nazis gave out free flags. Huge, blood-red swastika flags. And encouraged every family to hang out their flags in just such a way, at just the right angle, in front of their houses.

If a family didn't hang out a flag, the neighbors would start talking. "Hey, did you see that family down the street? They didn't have a flag out."

"Maybe a Communist? Maybe a Jew?"

The streets were ablaze with Nazi flags. An ocean of scarlet, every way you looked. And even as a Jewish kid who didn't know any better, I thought it was beautiful. Inspiring. It was like I was drowning in this sea of German pride and anger and emotion.

It didn't take long before things started to go downhill for our friends, our relatives and our family. At first, slowly. But then faster and faster, like a boulder tumbling down a mountain.

After a few months, the Nazi authorities decreed that Jews were not allowed to use public transportation any more. In the major cities like Cologne, we Jews became more and more restricted in what we could do, what jobs we could have and what businesses we could own.

A business owned by a Gentile, a non-Jew, would suddenly have a big swastika painted on its front window. A Jewish storekeeper would come to work in the morning and find a big star of David painted on his store. Along with a scrawled message: "We are Germans. We are proud. Don't patronize the Jews."

Hitler and his henchmen, Himmler and Goebbels and Goering, were using their skills of showmanship and propaganda, backed by the authority and visibility of the German state, to tell all of Germany that Jews were subhuman. That we were like rats. That we were vermin, a virus. And that if you didn't believe your leaders, you were suspect. Disloyal. A traitor. Not a true German.

The German people, it's sad to say, were more than happy to go along.

"They" are the problem, they were taught. Not "us". So let's attack "them". Vilify "them". Even kill "them".

Within a year or so, in 1935, the Nuremburg laws were declared.

Nazi Rally, Nuremburg, Germany, 1934

Chapter 5

Under Pressure.

At the 1935 Nazi Party Nuremberg Rally, a sweeping series of laws were enacted that brought into German law many of the anti-Jewish policies that were beginning to mess up our lives.

The laws revoked all Jews' German citizenship. It prohibited all "Aryans"——Germans with "pure" German blood—from having sex with Jews. It prohibited Jews from working in just about any profession—civil servants, lawyers, doctors and judges were now all out of work.

Jews like my father, who had served in the military and who received veterans' benefits, were suddenly cut off. The names of Jews who had died in World War I, fighting for Germany, were chiseled off the granite faces of war memorials in cities all across Germany.

And most devastating of all, Jews were not allowed to own their own businesses, in many cases businesses they had built from the ground up, for generation after generation. Jews were not allowed to own a house, a car, a newspaper or a magazine subscription. We were not allowed on the streetcars, in movie houses or theaters or even on park benches. Signs that said *"Juden Verboten"*—"No Jews Allowed"—popped up all over the city.

That was all gone, at the stroke of Hitler's pen.

My father walked into his company office the next day and found a Nazi official who had taken over sitting in his office, at his desk. My father was out, his accounts frozen, his business taken with no compensation.

There was no judge, no jury. Nothing. His whole life had been taken away, and there was nothing he could do about it. The judges—the non-Jewish judges, of course—suddenly started wearing Nazi pins on their lapels. They all joined the Nazi party. There was no doubt who was in charge, or how unjust the German justice system had become.

The Nazis forced us to hand in all our possessions: anything of value. They took my mother's jewelry, our silver, everything. One day, they came for our radio. There it went, our prized possession, gone out the door in the hands of a Nazi Brownshirt.

Jews could not meet, or assemble, in groups of more than three or four. We could not even attend our own Jewish community center.

We lost our apartment, of course. With my father's business gone, we had no income. We Jews were not allowed to own a home, and were not allowed to even live in an apartment that was owned by a Gentile.

After a struggle, we were able to find an apartment: a one-bedroom apartment in a much poorer part of Cologne. Our original home was Brabanterstrasse Number 12. We were forced to move to Flower Street— Blumenthalstrasse Number 15.

We had no way to see what horrors were coming. But at the time, it seemed quite horrible enough. In a period of a few weeks, our lives fell apart. We went from a prestigious street and a nice apartment to a cramped, miserable apartment: just one bedroom and a kitchen.

It was a huge blow. Imagine how you would feel if there was an angry knock on the door, and soldiers and bureaucrats barged in one day and took away your work, your citizenship, your possessions, and even your home.

It hit us all. It hit us like a ton of bricks. But it hit my father the worst. He fell into a severe depression. He was a successful man, a proud German, a war hero, a respected member of the community. But now he was nothing, at least in his own eyes.

He was forced into slave labor. He had to go away on the trains, to the west, to a Nazi labor camp, so he was away from us for most of every month. He was paid just a small amount of money for his work. One weekend every month he was allowed to come back home, to see us for a short time, and give us all the money he could, to give us a small chance to keep on going.

He told us he was working ten or twelve hours every day, building the fortifications for the German Army that would eventually be called the Siegfried Line. It was a huge system of concrete bunkers, tank traps and artillery positions the Nazis had designed to protect Germany from invasion from the west when the next war started. This line was directly across from the French Maginot Line—two immense networks of fortifications, stretching from north to south, that were supposed to protect France and Germany from each other.

With his small slave wages we had barely enough money to buy groceries, so we could just about feed ourselves when he was away. Food was increasingly scarce and expensive, so we learned quickly to eat less, and get by on worse food. We wasted nothing. We still felt like we were starving.

Our apartment was claustrophobic and cramped, even for our little family of three. We had it to ourselves for about three weeks. But before too long, it was about to get much more crowded. All our relatives in Cologne had lost their apartments as well. And since we were the only family with even a small place to stay, they all were forced to move in with us, one family at a time, as they were evicted from their rightful homes. At one point we had eleven people living there, all crammed together elbow to elbow. There was only one bed, so we were forced to sleep in shifts, two or three people at a time, on alternating nights.

In the kitchen, there was a little bare wooden bench. That was where I slept. And for short period of time I didn't even have that to myself—I had to share it, rotating places with Lore, a cousin of mine, a young girl who was jammed in with us. In 1936, the Germans also closed down even the Jewish schools. So the other kids and I had nothing to do, and pretty much nowhere in which to do it. People came and people left. Some of our relatives and friends managed to find a way out of this mess, to escape to another country.

Up until 1938, it was still possible, for some people, to find a way out of Germany. The process of getting out was very difficult. It's hard for us to understand now, in America, that in Germany at the time you actually needed permission to leave. Germany was a police state. Which meant that the government knew everything about every citizen. You couldn't go off for a vacation without registering in the new police department where you went. If you were gone for seven days, you had to register in the new place. Then re-register back home when you returned. The paperwork was insane—like something out of Franz Kafka.

The irony is that the original Nazi/German philosophy was to get rid of the Jews however they could. Initially, a great number of Jews were allowed to emigrate—the Germans were willing to kick us out however possible. Some people escaped to Palestine, to what is now Israel. Some managed to slip over the mountains into Switzerland. Some had special passports stamped with a big "J" for "*Jude*"—German for Jew. If you had one of those passports, you could leave Germany—but you could never come back.

Another problem was that in order to get out of Germany, you had to have a country that was willing to take you in. And none of the major countries in the Western world—including the United States—were willing to take in tens of thousands, even hundreds of thousands of Jews—Jews suddenly without property, money or jobs—that Germany didn't want. A very few countries allowed a limited number of Jewish refugees. Paraguay and Uruguay, in South America, allowed a few families to buy their way in. And some Jews—about 20,000—were allowed to stay in a cramped ghetto in Japanese-occupied Shanghai, China, due to the actions of some courageous Japanese and Chinese officials.

Some children were lucky enough to be sent on their own to countries that were, at the moment, safer for them than Germany. The *Kindertransport* was a heroic rescue mission, organized by the Central British Fund For German Jewry, which placed nearly 10,000 children in foster homes throughout Great Britain. Imagine sending your only child off to England, where you had never been, to be adopted by strangers for an indefinite period of time, on the suspicion that things were going to get even worse in Germany. This was, of course, the same England that my father had fought against in the first war, just 20 years before.

My father was required to stay in Germany because he was enlisted in the slave labor camps in the west. My mother and I couldn't just leave without him. We had no money, no resources, and no way to make it in the world on our own. As long as he was alive, and kept coming home to see us with a little food and a little money, we were still a family. And there's a nearly unbreakable bond that makes a family want to stay together as a family, no matter how hard or grim things get.

I wasn't allowed to go to a formal school, outside the apartment, anymore. But one of my former teachers did manage to slip in now and then and give me some private lessons, in Hebrew and other subjects, in preparation for my Bar Mitzvah. A Bar Mitzvah that I still, to this day, have never had.

We had to do this in the strictest secrecy. Everybody spied on everybody. The indoctrinated German children spied on their friends and families. They squealed on their own mothers and fathers. It was their patriotic duty to inform the Nazis against anyone.

"This person is suspicious. That person said something against the Fuhrer. This other person might be a Communist, or a traitor". All to get ahead a little, to get Nazi brownie points, to protect yourself against your neighbor, who is probably informing about you.

Chapter 6

A night to remember. A night to forget.

Throughout 1936 and 1937 things stabilized a little. Our lives were no better. We were hungry and cramped, bored out of our minds, frightened about our future and generally miserable.

Then the noose started to tighten. In 1938, the borders were officially closed. Jewish emigration was stopped completely. Germany was a fortified country. The borders were armed frontiers with watch towers, barbed wire and machine guns. Transportation, at least for us, didn't exist. We couldn't take the trains. Some people managed to slip out through the Jewish underground. There were a few routes that you could take. If you could find a horse, you might go over the mountains and end up in Switzerland. There were some escape routes, some possible ways out. But you had to be young and strong. I was too young, my mother was too old, and my father usually wasn't there with us. So my family and I were stuck. We didn't have the resources, or the luck, to get out. And there was no way of knowing just how bad things were going to get. All through the war—all through the Holocaust, in fact—there was this reluctance to believe that human beings could be so horrendous to each other. Even after the war. Even now, in fact. It's almost impossible to think about the things that were about to occur.

So guess what? We don't think about it. We find ways to pretend that it couldn't happen. That it will never happen.

That it never did happen.

The Nazis were becoming bolder and more brazen in their attacks, and in the propaganda that we'd see out on the streets every day. There would be marches and parades, proud Nazi SA stormtroopers, Hitler Youth and other groups, all itching for an excuse to kick around a Jew or anybody else who dared to stand up against them.

Then one night, as the nights were getting longer and the wind was getting colder, the whole city of Cologne seemed to go up in flames. It was the ninth of November, 1938.

We had no telephone, of course. That would have been illegal. When there was news, we heard it from mouth to mouth, through our neighborhood and the Jewish grapevine.

My mother, my father and I, and some of our relatives, were huddled up in our apartment that night. We could hear yelling, and glass storefronts smashing down on the streets. These were the sounds of the few remaining Jewish shops being surrounded by mobs, of their shop windows shattering into pieces on the sidewalks.

Up until that time, there were still some Jewish shops that were allowed to stay open, in order to feed and supply all the German Jews who were still living in those areas. But on November 9th, all over Germany, it was obvious that the Nazis had decided to make a show of just how ruthless they could be, and just how much they hated the Jews.

Relatives came running up the stairs to the apartment, breathless. "We can't believe what is happening! Everything is burning, burning, burning!"

I remember one older man, Gustav Heidt, a cousin of ours by marriage, coming up to tell us what was going on outside. He was an ugly man with terrible acne, about 50 years old. He saw himself as a guy who could get things done, a big man, a Jew who tried to find ways to get along with the Germans. But this night he was just as panicked as we were. He told us that the old city was burning. Anything Jewish was being torched. All the synagogues, the shops. He said the streets and the sidewalks were covered with the broken glass.

The city was filled with smoke, and as the night grew deeper we could see the orange flames and the crazy shadows bouncing off the buildings around us. People were running in panic. The city around us was being smashed to pieces.

That same thing was happening all over Germany, we later found out. The Germans always claimed that it was not planned, this countrywide attack on the Jews. But of course it was. The pretext the Nazis gave to the world was that the attack on all things Jewish that night, in both Germany and Austria, was a "spontaneous uprising" triggered by the death of a German diplomat, Ernst vom Rath, in Paris.

Vom Rath had been shot by a 17-year-old Jewish boy, Herschel Grynszpan, who was enraged by the treatment of his family by the Nazis. Brutally expelled from Germany, they had been stranded, with 12,000 other Polish Jews, at the Polish border by a standoff between the Germans and the Poles. Neither country would accept them, so they were caught in a state of limbo, kept alive in the winter by food and shelter provided by the Polish Red Cross. The family begged their young son Herschel, who had been stranded in Paris in an attempt to emigrate to Palestine, for any help he could provide. But he could not beg, borrow or steal any money to help resolve their situation. In a rage, he bought a gun with his last few francs, walked to the German Embassy, and shot the first embassy official he saw, Herr vom Rath.

Herschel gave himself up without protest to the French authorities. The shooting occurred on November 7th, but Vom Rath hovered near death until he finally succumbed on November 9th. Which also happened to be the 15th anniversary of the Beer Hall Putsch, Hitler's first attempt to take power in Germany.

When the German diplomat died, Nazi Propaganda Minister Joseph Goebbels gave a speech at the famous Bürgerbraükeller beer hall in Munich, blaming all the Jews of Europe for the actions of one enraged, frustrated 17-year-old boy. With Hitler's approval he goaded Nazi SA Stormtroopers and other thugs all over Germany and Austria to take the law into their own hands and attack Jewish businesses, community centers and synagogues.

It was as if the President of the United States had given a speech and said, "I think everybody who is a good American should ignore the law and the police, and go out and smash every black person, every black-owned business, and every Southern Baptist church they can find."

The dogs were let loose, in some cases literally. Nazi thugs roamed the streets, killing over 90 people. The police just stood by and let the SA, the *Schutstaffel* (SS), and all their Nazi friends tear apart the Jewish parts of every city.

It became known, the world over, as *Kristallnacht*—The Night of Crystal—because the shards of broken glass from the shattered shop windows gleamed like crystal in the dancing fire light.

Chapter 7

"This is a mistake!"

They came for my father around midnight.

That night, all throughout Cologne, and in other cities all over Germany, Jews were being arrested, rounded up in the dead of night from their apartments and dragged away.

There was an explosion of noise in the hall outside our apartment. The walls shook with the sounds of dogs barking, and enraged men yelling and banging on our door. The Germans forced the door open and we were assaulted with light and sound and fury: German Shepherds, and SS men with flashlights, pistols and unsheathed bayonets. We thought we were all going to die.

The leader of the raiding party stood silhouetted in the door. He was an SS officer in a black uniform, and a tall peaked hat with the SS death's-head symbol right in the middle. All my father could do was stand there, terrified. My mother and I, and our few relatives, could see around my father, to the soldiers and the dogs. It was a tiny one-room apartment, so we could all see what was going on in the doorway.

The officer took one look at my father, and then turned around to his squad of Nazi goons.

"This is a mistake," he barked at his men. And just as quickly as they had come, they left. My father stumbled back into the room with us, trying to catch his breath.

After a few minutes, as things calmed down in the apartment, my father told us why he thought he had been spared.

Part of my father's job, with his department-store company, had been to decide which products would be featured in the stores. He would meet with the various salesmen of all the wholesale products twice a year.

It was customary for each salesman to rent his own hotel room in the same hotel, to have a place to show his products. My father would then go from room to room inspecting the products and negotiating with the salesmen all in one place, so the salesmen wouldn't have to visit every store.

Every six months my father had gone to this same hotel in Cologne to do his buying for the upcoming season. He had tipped the doorman of the hotel a mark or two each time. Well, the SS officer who had come to take my father away, who now had so much power over our lives and the lives of other Jews, was that doorman. And he spared my father because of the ten or twelve Deutschmarks my father had tipped him over the years.

We found out later that the Nazis had arrested over 30,000 people that night. I don't know how the Nazis chose which men to pick up and take away. Those 30,000 were taken, for the most part, to become slave laborers working to enlarge the concentration camps, and to build new ones.

There were 13 concentration camps at the time. The Nazis were not yet using them specifically to kill people. They were used to house enemies of the state; political prisoners, mostly Communists, and anybody else they wanted to keep out of their hair, including clergymen, opposition writers and artists. But just as in the labor camps that were used to help fortify the German border, life in these camps was very hard.

The families and relatives of Jews who had been taken would often later get a postcard from the Germans, saying that their father or son or brother had died of *Lungenentzündung*. Which means an infection of the lungs, what we call pneumonia. Nobody ever seemed to die of anything else—it was always *Lungenentzündung*.

They might have been beaten to death by a guard, or shot for straying too near a fence, or crushed in a working accident. But when the postcard came, it was always "Your loved one died from *Lungenentzündung*". The laborers lived in tents, which were often wet, cold and rife with disease. So it was a semi-plausible reason that your father wouldn't be coming home. But the Nazis used it so often, it quickly became clear that they were attributing any death in the camps to it. Call it a convenient untruth.

As with the hotel doorman, some Germans would go out of their way, at least in the early days of the Nazi regime, to help Jews or Jewish families that they had formed friendships with over the years. It had a lot to do with how close they were to each other, how strong the connection was. But as time went on, it became more and more dangerous for Gentile Germans, no matter how well-intentioned they were, to help us.

Many Christians had been arrested as well, swept away in the night. The Nazis rounded up anybody whom they thought might ever oppose them, or be a threat to their rule and authority, so it wasn't just Jews who were being persecuted. They took political prisoners, Communists, homosexuals, and other groups, like Gypsies, away too. Anybody who didn't measure up to their crazy ideas of so-called Aryans being a master race.

"*Lungenentzündung*" became a cliché of the time. It was the euphemism, the code word, for the fear that the government, the Nazis, instilled in everyone. It was shorthand for the understanding all Germans had that if they stepped out of line—or even appeared to—they could be whisked away just like that, in the middle of the night, and never heard from again.

"I'd like to help you out", a German Gentile might say to a Jewish friend who had the courage to ask for help. "But there's a lot of *Lungenentzündung* going around."

Chapter 8

Nowhere to go. Nothing to do.

So my Dad escaped the raid on Kristallnacht. But that had been the end of his slave-labor job building the fortifications in the West. We were now just stuck in this tiny apartment, with nowhere to go and nothing much to do—no school and no work. We were only allowed outside in the daytime—there was a 6:00 PM curfew for Jews, ostensibly because at night, the police couldn't see the Jewish star on your jacket, and you might get away with doing something a Jew wasn't allowed to do.

Every now and then we would go to a friend's or a relative's house before the curfew and stay there—anything to break up the monotony. We would just sit around and commiserate. Somebody might go out for a little while and then come back with some food, or even smuggle an illegal newspaper in with the vegetables.

We would devour that newspaper, read every word. We would do anything to get news from the outside world. There were rumors flying everywhere, almost none of them based in real facts. When you have no idea of what is really going on, you make things up to fill the vacuum.

My father was growing even more depressed. There was an air of hopelessness all around us. It was a strange feeling, especially for him, not knowing what the next day would bring. And he suffered from not being able to provide for us, to protect us. He would sometimes come home with a bag of food and paper goods—I think they had been donated from abroad, maybe Jewish organizations in America, or other countries in Europe. But there wasn't much he could do to help us, and it weighed on him terribly. We could see his shoulders stooping, his face getting greyer, the light in his eyes dimming with each passing day.

He had always been a heavy smoker—this was, of course, back in the days when nobody realized just how dangerous and destructive smoking is.

But now he couldn't get real tobacco. It was too rare and much too expensive. So he took to smoking Chamomile tea, and just about anything else he could get his hands on. Leaves, weeds, anything. He would roll them up in pieces of newspaper and smoke away, disappearing in a noxious cloud. It was like he was smoking a campfire.

One of the people who lived with us for about three months, an older cousin named Walter, announced one day that he would try to escape. Walter had been captured on Kristallnacht and imprisoned in the Buchenwald concentration camp, near Weimar, Germany, forced with his fellow prisoners to help build and expand the place. But he had later been released, along with the luckier of those first Jewish prisoners.

Walter told us stories of how awful the conditions had been at Buchenwald, and how brutally he and his fellow Jews had been treated.

Because of the horrors he had witnessed, he was determined to escape from Germany, no matter how much he had to risk. We never knew—I don't know to this day—if he succeeded or not. He was just there one day, and gone the next. Chances are that he made it through to Switzerland. Because he was strong, and could travel alone, his chances were good. Because I never found out for sure, I chose to believe that he had gotten away.

Chapter 9

The Precious Shrapnel.

On September 1, 1939, Germany invaded Poland and started World War II—the second world war they had started in 25 years. So now, on top of everything else, we were suddenly in the middle of a war zone.

There was one strange sport that a couple of friends of mine and I invented to pass the time. We were still young boys, of course. Curious. Restless. And desperate for any adventure we could come up with, just to relieve the boredom.

Cologne has a huge railroad marshalling yard, right in the center of the city near the famous Dom cathedral. It is the hub for many of the railroads that connect the western part of Germany to central Germany and then to Poland and other countries of Eastern Europe. So it was a very strategic city, and because of that it was a favorite target for Allied bombers.

The British Royal Air Force, the RAF, and later the American Army Air Corps, bombed the hell out of the railroad yards, starting in May of 1940. They also hit the two main powerplants outside the city. In those days, bombers couldn't often actually hit what they were aiming at. So we had no idea of what was going to fall, and where it was going to hit.

I remember that the bombers' engines had different sounds. Some sounded smaller, with a higher pitch. We thought those were the British bombers. Later, the engine tones got lower and more powerful, and we thought that those were American planes.

In retrospect, I realize that they were all twin-engined British bombers—Bristol Blenheims, Hampdens, Armstrong Whitworths and later the bigger Wellingtons. The Americans hadn't even entered the war yet, and they had not started to supply bombers to the British. But even at that time we had the feeling that America was our last great hope. That America was coming to save us. I guess we were indulging in wishful thinking, hoping that the outside world knew what we were going through, and was trying to find some way to help.

With all the Jews now stuck in Germany, the Germans had to find a way to tell who was who. We were all forced to wear a yellow Star of David and the word *"Jude"* whenever we went outside the house.

We were required to wear a jacket with the yellow star sewn onto the left front and the back. It was like wearing a target. Before they put the stars on my jacket, I could often disappear into a crowd. Even if someone suspected I was Jewish, and wanted to give me trouble somehow, they could never be sure before.

Now there was no doubt. If a Nazi *Sturmabteilung (SA)* Brownshirt, a leather-coated thug from the Gestapo, or some Hitler Youth bad boy decided he wanted to show off to his buddies by roughing up a Jew, he knew exactly whom to pick on. "Beat the Jew" became the national pastime.

One day I was walking along the street, on the way to pick up a few vegetables for dinner for my mother, when a group of German boys grabbed me. They pulled me, screaming, into an alley. I thought I was dead. But instead of beating me, they started to pull off my pants. They were laughing at me, taunting me. What they were after, I soon realized, was a good long look at my very terrified, very circumcised Jewish penis.

Once they had satisfied their curiosity I managed to escape out onto the street, pulling up my pants as I ran away.

As mere Jews, not worthy of life or protection, we were not allowed in the air raid shelters where the German Gentiles hid at night during the air raids. And if a raid happened in the daytime, when we were actually allowed out on the streets, all we could do is hide the best we could, covering up to avoid being hit by a bomb, or flying bricks, or the falling steel fragments of anti-aircraft shells.

But being boys, we turned the aftermath of each bombing raid into our own bizarre game.

I would meet with a couple of like-minded friends—Herbert Levy, and another boy named Rolf—right after each night raid, first thing in the morning. I had an illegal coat that didn't have a Star of David on it, so every now and then I could slip around the city without being spotted and singled out as a Jew. It was dangerous. But it was fun.

We would meet very secretly, in a place we had picked out the night before. And act very cool, so we didn't attract any attention. The Germans were not that interested in us, after all. We were just 10- and 11-year-old kids, so we weren't much of a threat to anyone.

We raced around the city in the morning, competing to pick up the biggest, most fearsome-looking pieces of shrapnel. Some of these would be pieces of Allied bombs, we thought. But most were probably fragments of our own German anti-aircraft shells, raining down onto the city after they had exploded in mid-air.

A big piece of shrapnel was my pride and joy, in the bizarre value system of our scruffy little gang of scavengers. The chunks of twisted steel were always rusty by the time we picked them up in the morning. I guess there is something about the heat and corrosive nature of the explosives that causes them to rust almost instantly after they blow up.

Whoever found the biggest piece of shrapnel was the hero of the day. I remember the scent of the fragments, the smell of rust and iron and gun powder, the chemical residue from the blast. We would find the pieces in the strangest places—up on roofs, in back alleys, in trees, on top of carriages and trash cans.

Once we had gathered these pieces, these twisted chunks of iron and steel, we would trade them back and forth, like American kids trading marbles or baseball cards. The ultimate thrill was finding two fragments that fit together, like pieces of a jigsaw puzzle. That meant that they had come from the same shell or bomb, and for some reason we thought that was the most exciting thing we had ever seen.

Our parents thought we were nuts. They were struggling to keep us alive, but their sons were running around hunting for these remnants of the war that was threatening us, and just about everybody else in Europe.

We were determined to invent games and explore, and have whatever fun we could manage. We had nothing. Just a little food and a place to sleep at night, crammed into cramped apartments with our families. But even from that, we still found a way to escape our reality for a few hours and just be goofy boys on our own, on the run, chasing after useless bits of blown-up steel.

Chapter 10

Report for deportation.

Time passed slowly, because there was almost nothing to do. Then one day, in October of 1941, a Gestapo courier came to the apartment with an official notice. We were to report for "resettlement".

We were puzzled and bewildered. Crammed into our closet-like apartment room, we kept asking each other questions that none of us could begin to answer.

Where we were going? Was it going to be better? Could it be worse? We had no idea. Just stress, anxiety and dread. Our family, the Osters, had been selected to be kicked out of Germany. Some of the people in the apartment were going to stay behind. We were seldom given a reason why something was going to happen. And when there was a reason, it was more than likely to be a lie.

The Germans were great at making up stories about how great your new home was going to be, how you were going to get work, a better place to live, better food. But time after time, it turned out to be just another elaborate ruse, to con us into being cooperative.

We were ordered to report on Monday morning to a huge collection center in the middle of the city—it was like a convention center, with room for thousands of people. We were allowed to bring just one suitcase, for all three of us. No food was permitted. We were ordered to present ourselves, first thing in the morning, ready to travel to who knows where. Of course it was terrifying. We were being yanked from our home, our home city, away from all our friends and relatives, and sent on into what we knew would be a much more dangerous, more hostile world, completely at the mercy of the Nazis.

People sometimes ask me: "Why didn't you hide? Why didn't you leave?" Well, there was no way. There was nobody who could help us, and there was no place to go. The German Gentile population wouldn't hide

Jews—it would be putting their necks on the line, just like ours. Some Catholic nuns and priests did whatever they could, usually for Catholic families that had intermarried with Jews, but there were way too many Jews and other persecuted people for them to help us all. If you had the right connections and resources, and luck, maybe you could find a way to hide, or escape. We had none of those.

And as Germans, we were pretty much programmed to fall into line, to behave in an orderly, law-abiding way. It's part of the German culture: if our government says we are supposed to do something, we do it. That was one of the reasons the German people fell into the grip of the Nazis so easily. To the German way of thinking, if you don't follow the law, you're a criminal. And unlike here in America, where there's a bit of sexiness, sometimes, to being outside the law—think of Jessie James, or Bonnie and Clyde—in Germany that's not how people think. At least not back then.

Germans tend to do what their government tells them to do. And we were Jews, of course. But first, we were Germans. I know how odd that sounds now, knowing how it all turned out. Knowing that so many millions of people were murdered. But that was how it was at the time. In retrospect, Adolf Hitler was the criminal, one of the greatest criminals of all time. But at the time he was, more or less, the legitimate head of state of Germany. So there was a natural reluctance to go outside the law, even when the law seemed to be stacked against us. It was like when my Dad went over the top of the trenches in World War I. He knew he might be killed. He had seen his friends and colleagues butchered by machine guns and poison gas and artillery fire all around him, for months on end. But he had been indoctrinated to believe that dying for his country was the right thing to do.

We were resigned to reporting on Monday. But late on Saturday night the Germans came to our crowded apartment again. They had apparently decided that if we were going to run, to attempt to avoid our deportation on Monday, they were most likely to catch us, unprepared, a couple nights before.

Just as it was on Kristallnacht, we woke up to the same ear-shattering, terrifying drama scene. Soldiers banging on the door. Bright flashlights in our faces, blinding us. German Shepherds, snarling, teeth bared, straining at their handler's leashes.

I've noticed, over the years, that African-American kids brought up in the 60s and 70s are especially afraid of dogs, particularly German

Shepherds. Well, that is because they were brought up watching the police in Mississippi and Alabama threaten black people and civil rights protesters with "police dogs". They saw their fathers, their brothers, their uncles and their cousins, attacked and mauled on their black-and-white TVs.

I know just how they feel. You can argue with a man. You might reason with him. But you know damn well that you can't talk sense to a crazy, wolf-like German Shepherd. The Germans burst through the door and into our apartment. They ordered us out of our home. Right here. Right now. They herded us down the stairs and into the street, threatening us with rifles, pistols, bayonets and dogs. All we had were each other, and the few belongings we could grab as we were hustled out the door and down the stairs.

I remember that they took us, with one other couple, and dragged us down to the street. The Germans always preferred to do their dirty work in the dark. It was their ally, because late at night you're confused, you're sleepy, you can't see straight. And so you're much less likely to resist. We were taken to the collection center near the railroad station, where we all milled around, not knowing what was going to happen to us. There must have been 1000 people there, all crammed together.

We had no food, and the Germans didn't give us any—all they gave us was water. Some people had smuggled some candy into their suitcases, and that night it was like gold, some of the luckier people feeding the kids, like me, whatever they had. It was like the Superdome in New Orleans during Hurricane Katrina—chaos, depression, and a sense of futility. Desperate people all piled in together, without food, not knowing what was going to happen.

The next day they loaded us onto a small train, with just a few passenger cars. We were all locked inside, with no way to escape. There was enough room to sit for some people, but some had to stand—we rotated so everybody could sit some of the time, and then take a turn standing.

We were locked into the train for a couple days, rocking and screeching east across Germany, and then into Poland. The conditions were awful. There were not enough toilets for all these people, so very soon the cars smelled like latrines. There were children crying. Babies screaming. Shocked mothers and fathers trying to reassure their kids that everything was going to be all right, even though we were sure that it was going to be anything but all right.

Finally, we pulled into a dirty, unkempt city. The people on the streets looked even more miserable than we felt. They were unshaven, clothed in tattered rags. They looked starved, beaten and exhausted.

"Where are we?" asked a man from the train, as we pulled into the station.

"You're in Poland, in the city of Lodz," said a walking skeleton on the platform.

"Welcome to the ghetto."

Chapter 11

One room. 21 people.

From the train, we were herded into an another assembly area. Eventually the ghetto police, Jews who were indirectly collaborating with the Nazis, divided us up into groups and gave us an address to go to for our housing.

Compared to Germany, Poland was a very underdeveloped country, with great poverty even before the war. The Germans shoved us into these primitive apartment houses which were really just brick buildings with rooms, nothing more. There were no bathrooms, no running water, gas, heat or furniture. Some of the windows had been shattered, leaving us exposed to the cruel Polish winter in the middle of October.

When we first arrived there it was so cold that if you spit, your saliva would freeze before it hit the ground. These ghetto police shoved 21 people, including my father, my mother and me, into one room the size of a child's bedroom.

The entire ghetto held 160,000 people. These were jammed into just 20,000 rooms, many of which were not habitable. The floors were split open, the walls were crumbling. It was like a tornado had torn through the city. Many of the structures were simply falling apart.

The Germans had cordoned off sections of Polish cities to serve as improvised concentration camps for Jews while the real camps were being built out in the countryside.

The Lodz ghetto was the second largest: the biggest was in Warsaw, the Polish capital.

Just as in Venice and Rome in the fourteenth century, the Lodz Ghetto was walled off from the rest of the city. The Germans did it with electric fences and barbed wire, with guard towers and machine guns every few hundred feet.

There was one strange feature of the Lodz Ghetto. The streetcar tracks ran right through the middle of the ghetto and free, Gentile Poles could ride right through on their way from one side of the ghetto to the other. To connect the two sides of the Ghetto, the Germans built a wooden bridge over the tracks, and lined it with barbed wire to keep the Jews from escaping down the train line.

So you had this strange nether world, where the two communities came into contact with each other. We Jews along the fence could see these better-dressed, better-fed Poles and others riding along just a few feet away, enclosed in their safe, clean street cars. And the Gentiles could

Photo: U.S. Holocaust Memorial Museum Archive

Imprisoned Jews crossing the Ghetto bridge over the streetcar tracks; Lodz, Poland.

see us, of course, at least in the early days of the Ghetto—the starving, grey-faced, miserable Jews. It didn't take long before my mother, my father and I looked just as hungry and disheveled as the Jews we saw that first day as our train rolled into Lodz.

The streetcar track running through the Ghetto was like a train of gawking tourists, riding through a cruel, overcrowded zoo.

Later on in the war, the Germans actually painted the windows of the street cars, so that the free people of Lodz couldn't see how terrible the conditions were becoming for us starving grey Jews behind the wire.

There was a Jewish government—the *Judenrat*—in the Lodz ghetto, run by Mordechai Chaim Rumkowski, a self-important Jew who had decided to collaborate with the Germans. He thought that by organizing the ghetto himself, using other cooperative Jews, he could stave off the "transports" to the concentration camps in the East, which he knew were essentially slave-labor camps and extermination camps for the young, the weak, the sick and the undesirable. He was autocratic and tyrannical, and his close ties to the Nazis made most of the Jews in the Ghetto resent him, his slavish acceptance of German orders, and the horrible tasks he was forced to carry out.

Photo: U.S. Holocaust Memorial Museum Archive

Jewish children line up for soup in the Lodz Ghetto, Lodz, Poland.
Of 204,000 Jews who passed through the Lodz Ghetto, only about 10,000 survived the war.
Children of this age were typically taken from their parents and sent to be murdered
at the Chelmno, Poland extermination camp.

It was Rumkowski, not the Germans, who decided who would stay and work in Lodz, and who would be shipped off to the East. The Germans would give him a quota, a number of people to be transported. But it was he who decided exactly who would go. It was he, in essence, who would decide who would live, and who would probably die.

Rumkowski believed that the Jews' best chance for survival was to organize and create a wide variety of industries within the ghetto, all designed to supply the Germans and the German war effort. By making the Ghetto self-sufficient, even creating a profit for the Germans, he reasoned that he could postpone, or possibly even prevent, the Ghetto being "liquidated". That is, he might be able to keep more Jews alive longer by becoming the Germans' apparent allies, rather than their enemies.

The Rumkowski administration also organized many of the Lodz Ghetto's institutions, aimed presumably at making life better, if possible, for us inmates. The *Judenrat* established primitive hospitals, some schools, and organized the slave labor assignments to keep the Ghetto producing as much as possible.

He did succeed in preserving the Lodz Ghetto longer than any other Jewish Ghetto in Poland, possibly saving lives by delaying the inevitable transports to extermination camps. The Lodz ghetto was the only one that was not run directly by the Nazi SS, so even though conditions in the Ghetto were barbaric, it is also possible that some Jews were saved by having less-frequent contact with the murderous, trigger-happy Nazis.

But we knew nothing of this when we arrived. We were just three miserable, hungry, dirty, penniless Jews, doing our best to survive the present, all the while dreading our future.

Chapter 12

The calculus of soup.

Within a few days, my father and mother were given their work assignments. The ghetto police had explained to us that if we had work, we would get extra rations of food, so my parents were eager to have jobs. There was nothing to do if you didn't work, and none of us were eager to spend any more time than necessary in our horrible, stinking room, crammed from floor to ceiling with cranky, complaining strangers.

My mother was forced to work in a factory that made *Stiefelplatten*—the little iron toe and heel plates for Germans' jackboot soles that make the leather last longer. These were the plates that made the sound of marching Germans so loud and so menacing—there's no sound in the world like that of a hundred German soldiers, goosestepping in unison on a hard cobblestone street.

My father was ordered to work repairing the ghetto fence, fixing the posts, the barbed wire and the electric wire wherever it was broken through, or fell into disrepair.

What saved us from going straight to an extermination camp—like Chelmno or Treblinka—was a letter from the Kaiser my father had saved, which detailed his war service and the medals he had won. That letter saved us from near-certain death, I learned later. Chelmno, which was just 50 miles away, had no factories or even prisoner barracks, because almost no prisoners transported from Lodz survived their first day there. They were forced to undress, pushed into trucks, gassed with the trucks' exhaust, and then buried or burned in the nearby forest.

I was desperate to find work, mostly to get the extra rations, but also to have something to do, and to have more opportunities to find food. I figured, just like everybody else around me, that the more valuable I was to the Germans, the more likely it was that I'd be allowed to stick around. I was put into the ghetto work camp shortly before my 13th birthday, right before I was supposed to have my Bar Mitzvah. So I never had one, after all those years of memorizing the Torah, of studying Hebrew in secret.

If you didn't work, you didn't get your ration of soup in the middle of the day. I remember having my own aluminum bowl like everybody else. It was the most precious thing I owned. If you didn't have a bowl, you couldn't get your soup. So I punched a hole in the rim, looped a piece of string through the hole, and wore the bowl around my neck.

Once a day, at noon, workers would bring these old-fashioned milk cans from the communal kitchen, with a big ladle to serve the soup. And it became a deadly game, a weird sort of dance, to figure out where to stand in line to get the most nourishing pieces of vegetables.

You didn't want to be at the front of the line, because all the good parts of the soup would settle to the bottom, and all you would get would be liquid. And you didn't want to be at the end of the line, because there was no guarantee that if this can ran out, there would be another.

Some of the older guys taught me to calculate how many ladles of soup there were in each can. And then maneuver in the line so I got one of those last few ladles at the bottom, the ones with more vegetables, a few more calories. I was happy to find a leaf of cabbage. Coming across a nub of a potato was like winning the lottery.

That's why I was so desperate to work. To get an extra meal during the day, one more meal that I didn't have to scrounge or steal by myself.

Some kids my age didn't work, but I was determined. I tried to get a job at a furniture factory, working on a lathe and making wooden legs for tables and chairs, but that only lasted one day.

On the way home from that first day at work, I saw my mother's cousin, Jacob Levy, who had been a farmer back in Germany. I'm not sure of where he lived before he was transported to Lodz—I think his farm had been in the Frankfurt area.

"What are you doing?" he asked me. "I didn't know you were stuck here like me." He told us he had been here for three months, and he said he had found a good job, a good place to work.

"Don't worry," he said. "I can help you out. Meet me on the street corner here tomorrow morning, and you come with me. "

I had no idea of what he was talking about, or what was going to happen.

"Don't ask any questions," he said.

It turned out that Jacob was a big shot in the ghetto. The Germans needed a farming expert, and he was just the right guy for the job. He was a rough, tough farmer. A short little guy, but strong and rugged. The Germans were trying to grow as much food as possible inside the Ghetto, so they wouldn't need to supply the Jews from the outside. They liked working with him because he spoke German. They could communicate easily with him, unlike most of the Polish Jews in the Ghetto, who spoke only Polish and Yiddish.

He was a rare bird, a German Jew who was also a farmer. Making a living outdoors, in the fields, was not high on the list of preferred professions for most Jews at the time. He was in charge of this small farming project—a large field within the ghetto wire. He accepted me as one of the farm workers. So snap, just like that, I had a daytime job, for 12 hours every day.

There was another man who helped me out. His name was Erich Marx, and he was from Cologne like us. He was a very striking, imposing man, and he became the foreman of the people who were working on the farm with me.

My mother, my father and I would meet with the others in our room at night and exchange information, any rumors that we had heard when we were out at work during the day.

Some people had saved some of their most precious possessions: watches, jewelry, precious stones and rings that they had sewn into their clothing. There was a black market, of course, so little by little they would sell off things to the Polish Jews, who could sell them to the German guards, to buy a little extra food. I remember one woman sold a beautiful ring for a pound of potato peels, leftovers and garbage that had been smuggled out of the communal soup kitchen.

As each night fell, we all crouched along the walls of the room, our backs against the wall and our legs folded up in front. We would take turns in the night, one of us lying down for an hour or so while the others sat up.

There was no bathroom—just an outhouse. In the winter, when the outhouses filled up, we had to go nearby, out in the cold. There were these piles of feces, frozen in the gutters, from all these people jammed into the rooms. In the summer, you would try to go somewhere outside, and then the waste would be hosed away into the open street gutters. But no matter what season it was, it was a stinking, filthy, desperate way to live. It was also a perfect way to spread disease.

As a kind of relief, my father would still smoke whenever he could, whatever he could scrounge. So naturally I, Mr. Wise Guy, decided to give it a try when nobody was looking. Like most boys I looked up to my father. Smoking made him seem cool, and adult, and very impressive.

If my father did it, it had to be the right thing to do.

I found some chamomile and some other weeds, and rolled them up like my father did. I took one big puff, inhaled it, and promptly fell right over, knocked out like somebody had turned off a light switch. My parents found me like that, unconscious, laid out on the floor like a salmon at the fish market.

Chapter 13

The Ghetto Runner.

Working in the farm field was almost a relief. It was hard, but at least I was outdoors, away from all the people and the noise and the stench, doing something useful.

Obersturmbannführer Schwind, the Gestapo man in charge of the farm and food production, was a portly man, a plainclothes SS officer in those black leather coats they always wore. He didn't torture me or the other prisoners, but he was always yelling and screaming, because that's the German way to give a command.

He got along with my mother's cousin, Jacob, because they spoke the same language. Schwind must have been in the agriculture business before the war, because he knew a lot about it.

He also oversaw the distribution of the seeds and the seed potatoes. The potatoes were rigorously counted—God forbid, a Jew getting enough to eat. We had to cut them into quarters to plant, and we dealt with the other seeds—beans, peas, lentils and corn.

Schwind wore a Tyrolean hat, with the little feather in the band. One day he showed up, barking orders to everyone. He had found out that I spoke German. So he took me by the arm and said, "Boy—gonna make you the runner. You take each day's field report. If I don't come by 4 in the afternoon, you bring it over to the German administration building." So I had to drag myself across the ghetto and across the bridge over the streetcar line, every other day or so. He even got me a bicycle to help me make better time—I had it for three or four months.

I remember that the bike was rotten and rusted, but it was a big thing to me, being so important that I had my own bicycle. I didn't have the strength to pedal it very hard. Three or four days a week I rode it to the bridge, left it there, and walked over to leave the report. Then I had to pedal back to the field, to get back to work.

I didn't get any rewards for being the runner, but it was good in one respect. It gave me the time, and the freedom of movement, to steal a few bits of food now and then. If the harvest came in, I could steal some vegetables, or grab a couple of potatoes before they were counted.

My pants were "knickerbockers", with the bottoms of the legs tied above my ankles, over my stockings. I had torn a hole in each of my pockets, so when I managed to "organize" a little food, I would let it go through the pocket and down into the pants, where the Germans wouldn't find it when they patted us down every night.

Sometimes, I would bury the pieces of seed potatoes in the corner of a field. Then later, in the dark of night, I would go back and dig them up. That's how hard we had to work to survive. If I got caught, I would be killed. Even if we had a potato, the tragedy was that we had no fire to cook it.

We gathered splinters of wood from carving up the rafters, bit by bit, up in the attic. My mother, my father and I would sneak out in the night and make a fire, and we roasted that potato, huddled in a corner, hidden from everybody else. We couldn't do it in the room, because we would set the place on fire. We would have been forced to share it with the other people. And there just wasn't enough to go around.

I used to take a little shortcut through the fields, on my way back and forth with the reports. This was Poland in the winter, and there was deep snow everywhere on the ground. I discovered, by burrowing around where the cabbage had been harvested, that cabbage plants grow these little cabbages—like brussels sprouts—on their stalks under the snow.

Eating the few brussels sprouts was good. But the sprouts also attracted a few rabbits. I could see their tracks in the snow. Now a rabbit would be wonderful to catch. But how?

I talked it over with another boy who was working on the field with me. He devised a way to leave a sprout as bait, and looped a string around the sprout, so when a rabbit came it would get the string around its neck, and maybe strangle itself.

In all the time we tried, he only got one rabbit. But he never told me about it, and he never shared it with me. One day I went to see how the rabbit trap was doing, and I found the blood on the snow where he had killed it and eaten it.

It was survival of the fittest. Which was simply the way it was. I'm not sure that I would have shared it with him if I had gotten there first.

Chapter 14

The Sounds In The Night.

We were miserable, but because we had only been there a relatively short time, we were in better condition than the people who had come before. People aged very fast in the ghetto. Your life expectancy was about six months, because of the lack of food, the backbreaking work and the disease that ran through the neighborhoods. Imagine 21 people in a small room all night. If one person got sick, everybody got sick.

When the time ran out on the people in any particular neighborhood of the Ghetto—when they became thinner, weaker and less productive— they would disappear.

We could hear these raids in the distance, almost every night. We could hear sirens, dogs barking, and the clatter of the Germans' boots. We could hear the roar and rumble of trucks. We never heard trucks in the daytime, because the Germans were using horses in all the routine, day-to-day activities, to preserve the trucks and save the gasoline for tanks and airplanes. So when we heard the trucks in the middle of the night, we knew something was up.

Twice we heard the raids in the night, and woke up to find whole blocks of the ghetto deserted. We never knew what happened to these people.

Now, with all the research that's been done on the Lodz Ghetto, the concentration camps and the Holocaust, we know that Lodz was essentially a waiting room for death. The Germans had decided that nearly everyone who was sent to Lodz in that time was destined to be killed in one of the huge extermination camps: Chelmno, Treblinka or Auschwitz.

Those camps had only so much capacity. Capacity for the living—or capacity for killing and disposing of our bodies. So Lodz and the other ghettos were holding areas for the Nazis, a place to store the Jews of

Europe until our turn came to die. The Germans would try to get as much work out of us, where ever we were, of course—they had an incredible need for slave workers to produce food, and uniforms, and war material of every kind from boots to bullets to bombers.

But they had calculated very carefully just how long it was worth it to keep a Jew alive. For a few months, even under cruel, near-starvation conditions, a Jew could be of some use to the war effort. But once our health—and our will to work, our will to live—began to deteriorate, it was time to ship us out for extermination, and bring in a new group of men, women and children to fill our places.

Photo: U.S. Holocaust Memorial Museum Archive

Children at slave labor in the Lodz wood shop. Henry Oster, 13, worked here for one day before finding a job on the Ghetto farm.

Chapter 15

Fatherless Child.

My father's job maintaining the Ghetto fence was tough, and very dangerous. The Germans had guard towers all along the fence, with trigger-happy soldiers ready to shoot at anything that moved. If you got too close to the fence—even if it was your job to repair it—they were likely to shoot.

This took a big toll on him. He was being worked without mercy, and he and his co-workers were often being shot at by the Germans. A friend of my father's was killed that way. He was shot in the head by a guard because he was caught reaching through the fence to get a package that had been left there on the other side.

My father had been slightly wounded himself. He came home from work one afternoon bleeding from a gunshot wound in his arm. There had been an opening in the fence, and when he was forced out there to work on it by a stupid foreman, a guard in a nearby tower had shot at him, thinking that he was trying to escape through the hole. The guards were trained to shoot if they saw anything out of the ordinary. If a prisoner escaped, the guard was in big trouble. But if they shot somebody by mistake—no problem. After all, it was not as if they were shooting at a real human being. It was just a Jew.

My father's wound didn't seem that serious—a graze, through the fleshy part of his arm. He had been wounded before, in World War l, so he toughed it out—he acted as if it was no big deal. My mother cleaned the wound, bandaged it up, and my father went to work the next day. He had no choice. If he didn't work, he got no food. And we were all right on the edge of starvation as it was.

About a month later, he came home early from work. He had felt even weaker than usual, so he had been allowed to come home an hour or so before his usual quitting time. I remember him saying: "I'm so tired," when he came in.

My father had been worked so hard, for so long, that he had been slowly starving for months. And he had suffered from really crippling depression. He had been a strong, successful man, a well-respected part of our community. He had built an impressive career. But when the Nazis took all that away—took his job, his home, his ability to protect us—it was as if a spark had gone out inside him.

The day he came home early, he was so weak he had trouble climbing up to our room. He said, "God, I could hardly make the staircase, I'm so exhausted."

I was standing near a sleeping place on the floor—we didn't have a bed, so he had to lie on the floor, on a blanket we shared with the other people in the room. I had no idea how sick he really was. I was there watching over him, with my mother and two other women, a couple of family friends.

My mother cried out, "Hans, Hans." And he didn't respond. He just looked up at the ceiling, his eyes wide open. He gurgled, deep in his throat.

My mother realized that he wasn't breathing. She whispered to me, as gently as she could, "*Er ist weg*". "He is gone". It was quiet, simple, undramatic. He was just not there anymore.

We were sick with grief and horror and shock.

So now our big problem—other than losing my father—is this. What do you do with a corpse, in the Lodz Ghetto?

We had to do it ourselves—my mother, our friends and I. We had to pick up my father from his place on the floor, and take him down the stairs and out the front door. Then we put his body next to the gutter, as gently as we could.

We were forced to leave him there overnight, by the same gutter where the sewage ran, where people threw their waste. There was nothing else we could do—that was the official procedure for dealing with dead bodies in Lodz. We left my father out in front of our house and then trudged back up the stairs, heartbroken, to wait out the night, knowing he was lying out there, dead and alone.

When we took him outside he was still wearing the clothes he had been wearing when he died. But in the morning, he was naked. The people of Lodz were so desperate for anything to wear, for anything of any value, that they had stolen his clothing.

In the morning—every morning—a wagon came by to pick up the

dead. There were always dead.

I watched these two guys hop off the wagon, grab my father by the arms and legs, and throw him up on the cart. He was there, his arms hanging down, on this pile of bodies, all of them covered with the feces and the filth from the gutter.

We followed along behind the wagon as it bounced down the cobblestones. My mother and I walked in this awful little procession to see where his body was going to wind up.

When we got to the cemetery, the guys pushing the cart walked around to the front, tilted it up, and sent the emaciated, grey bodies tumbling out in a heap, arms and legs all tangled together. The scene was like a very real painting of hell. But with a gagging, horrifying smell. A smell that was made even more unbearable, knowing that my father was lying there in front of us, dumped like a dead dog.

All we could do then was leave him that way, turn around and go home. One of the cemetery workers told us that there would be a burial in the morning, because the Jewish religion requires burial the next day unless it's the Sabbath. So after a night of sobbing and grieving we came back the next morning. They had shrouds for the bodies, made out of cheesecloth. One of the workers asked us: "Which one is yours?"

"That's him," my mother said, pointing.

They dragged him out of the pile and wrapped him up. Then two of them grabbed him between them, and gave him a heave down into a hole. One of the men was kind enough to say a kaddish—a prayer for the departed. But there was no ceremony, no rabbi, no nothing.

I was not allowed to say kaddish myself, because I was not yet a man—I had not yet had my Bar Mitzvah.

I remember that my mother was so traumatized that she didn't say kaddish either. We both felt guilty about that. We felt that we had not done what was expected of us, by our religion and our traditions. We felt we had failed as a family. We were just too shocked, and numb, and horrified to do much of anything, I guess.

The men shoveled the earth onto his body. There was no marker, no nothing. Just a pile of dirt on the ground.

If this cemetery is still there today, I think I could find the spot where they buried my father. It was very close to the fence at the edge of the cemetery. There were rows and rows of toppled, broken gravestones. The Germans thought it was fun to kick the stones over, to desecrate the grave markers of the Jews.

In researching this book, we found the official German record of my father's death in the books from the Lodz Ghetto hospital. Which is ironic, now, because he never went to the hospital—he had simply come home one day, laid down on his blanket, and died. His cause of death was listed as "bronchial catarrh" or pneumonia. I don't remember a doctor or any other medical people coming to the house, but it's likely that after he passed away, the local ghetto authorities came and got the information about how he had died from my mother, or somebody else in the room.

Now it was just my mother and me.

Chapter 16

The Kindness of the Hangman.

One of my jobs on the ghetto farm was to climb up into the trees to pick cherries that had been forgotten in the harvest. The cherry trees were planted outside the cemetery wall, and they posed a unique challenge. The Germans would search us after work, so it was too dangerous to smuggle cherries back to our room. If I ate one while I was up in the tree, and was careless enough to drop a pit to the ground, I was done. Nobody else had been up in that tree, so the Germans would know that the pits had come from me.

I developed a technique of eating the cherry without taking it off the stem. I would find a place, high in the tree, concealed by the leaves. When I thought it was safe, I could quickly nibble around the pit, like a squirrel with a nut. The pit would wind up still hanging on the stem, up in the tree where nobody could see it. And if somebody did see it, I could blame it on the birds.

If the tree I was picking turned out to be close to the wall of the cemetery, I could throw the pits out, one at a time, over the stone wall and into the cemetery.

After about six months in the Ghetto, I started to become friends with a couple of Polish guys—a pair of brothers—who also worked on the farm with me. These two fellows had a lot of different jobs. They knew how to run a farm, and I tried to learn as much from them as I could. It was pretty obvious that unlike me they actually had some idea of how a farm worked. We weren't really friends, because I was so young and small compared to them. I was almost a mascot, like a stray puppy they had adopted.

They were tough, muscular characters. The older brother was big, strong and mean-looking, with huge shoulders. A real bruiser. His younger brother was just as menacing, but quite a bit shorter. So I figured it was good idea for me to stay on their good side, to try be their friend. A tiny kid like me certainly didn't want to be their enemy.

After I'd known them for a few weeks, they began to give me a slice of bread once in a while. I could sneak the bread back into the room at night, eat a few bites myself, and share it with my mother when everybody else in the room was asleep. The extra bread always came on a Monday, for some reason. I didn't ask why. We were so glad to get it. I just wanted to make sure I maintained my relationship with these tough guys who were helping to keep us alive.

We were not forced to work on Sundays. But one Sunday in particular, the Germans and Ghetto police came around to our neighborhood all of a sudden, herding us out of our rooms.

At first we thought that this was a raid, but this time in the daytime. We were panicked. The Germans tried to calm us down a bit, though we knew we could never trust them. They said, "No, it's not a raid. Just go over there to the field. You're going to see an attraction." The way they talked, with their cruel sense of humor, we could have been going to watch a puppet show.

We were, for the first time, being forced to watch what the Germans called Sunday's Entertainment. Other sections of the Ghetto had been forced to watch this, and had told us about it. But this was the first time our street had been subjected to it.

We were marched out into an unplanted field. There was a rough wooden gallows—a hanging platform, with three nooses strung from a beam—erected in the center. Now we understood what was going to happen. Jews who had broken a rule, or who were unlucky enough to be accused by a German SS or Gestapo man, were going to be hung. And we were going to watch, whether we wanted to or not.

Through the Ghetto grapevine, we knew all about it, in an abstract way. We had known who had been hanged each week, what they had been accused of, even which SS guard or leather-coated Gestapo thug had sent them to their death.

But today, it was much more than a whispered rumor. It was very real. We looked up and saw three miserable Jews, their hands tied behind their backs, who were waiting to die. Each victim was forced, in turn, up the stairs. I remember one had to be pulled up like a cloth dummy, his paralyzed feet refusing to carry him. A huge, heavy-set man held each victim while another dropped the noose over his neck. The man who had handled the noose then read the name of the condemned person, along with the crime they had supposedly committed: Stealing a carrot from the Reich. Disobedience to a German. Trying to escape. The had paper signs hung over their necks, saying who they were and what they had done.

One by one, the men were dropped. Their necks snapped sideways as they hit the end of the rope, their bodies bouncing up as the rope stretched and snapped back. The crowd around us gasped and moaned and cried. The hanged bodies jerked and convulsed for a few agonizing seconds. And then they were still, gone, just twisting.

I was in the back of the crowd. I was petrified. And not at all eager to be close to the gallows. So it took me a minute or two to get the courage to look up and really see what was happening, up there on the platform. With a shock, I recognized the two men up on the gallows. The hangmen were my two friends, the two tough Polish brothers. They were the well-fed men who had been slipping me extra bread, the bread that was helping to keep my mother and me going, week after week.

I realized why they always gave us their extra bread on Mondays. It was their extra pay for hanging their fellow Jews on Sunday.

The next morning, they slipped me the extra slice of bread, just as before. They didn't say a word about where it had come from. I guess they gave it to us to ease their consciences a little bit.

I didn't ask. Just as I had the Monday before, I took the bread home and shared it with my mother.

Chapter 17

The Secret In The Attic.

One hot, humid night in July, 1943, the Germans came for us. It was a raid, just as we had heard in the other sections of the ghetto. Like so many before us, we had been selected to disappear.

The Nazis planned these things very carefully. When a group had been in the Ghetto long enough so they were getting weaker, more starved, more depleted, they would round them up and ship them away. Then they would replace the used-up slaves with new arrivals, Jews from the occupied countries, people who were presumably in better shape. Just the way we had replaced the exhausted, hopeless Jews who had come before us.

One minute we were asleep. The next, the street was filled with noise and blinding light and chaos. First, we heard the roaring trucks and cars down on the cobblestones. Barking German Shepherds. Then the heavy banging of soldiers in jackboots, running up the stairs in every building, banging on doors, yelling at the top of their lungs.

"Get up, Jew! Move, move, move! Over here! No, over there! *Schnell! Schnell! Schnell!*"

Most of the soldiers were Germans, the SS. But some were Polish Army guards, captured Poles who had chosen to collaborate with the Germans, rather than being shot or starved to death. It didn't matter to them, or to us. They were the enemy now.

As we slowly walked out of our room, in a sad, shuffling line, I held my mother back a bit. I had explored the room in the previous months, trying to figure out how we might escape if a raid came for us. I thought I had an idea.

For a few moments, as our fellow room dwellers trundled down the stairs, dragging their few belongings, my mother and I were alone.

Just above the front door, above the transom, was a trap door that led to a small attic space. I stepped on the door handle, raised myself up on the edge of the transom and pushed the trap door open. Once I was up there, I could reach down and grab my mother's hands, so I could pull her up with me. I was thin, but she weighed almost nothing by then.

As quiet as burglars, we slid the trap door back into place and crawled over the dusty, spider-webbed rafters, fumbling in the dark toward the back of the attic.

I had been shaving off the tops of the rafters with a knife as the months went by, using the splinters of the beams for our tiny cooking fires. But toward the back, there was one taller rafter that we hadn't started carving yet.

We slid back behind that taller beam, in the narrow corner where the roof met the rafters, lying as flat and as quiet as we could in the rat droppings and filth. From there I could peer out under the eaves of the roof. Down on the street, I could see soldiers herding our room mates up and into the truck beds: men, women and their children. Some of them hoisted suitcases up with them, trying to save a few clothes and valuables.

The Germans, thorough as always, came looking for us. One of them got the idea to check the attic. We heard the trap door thump and slide, and felt the glow and flicker of light around us as he stuck his head up, probing with his square tin flashlight. We thought he was sure to see us or hear us. We could hear him, just a few feet away, breathing hard from the exertion of climbing up and sticking his head through the trapdoor. All we could do was lie there, trying to be invisible. Finally, after what had seemed like an hour, he gave up and dropped down to the hallway with a thump.

We heard him stomp down the stairs. The yelling, the crying, and the metal clatter of hobnails and rifles died down. We let ourselves breathe a little. We could hear the trucks starting up and rolling away, the sick-sweet exhaust fumes from their engines filtering into the attic through the open eaves.

After an hour or so, when we were pretty sure the Germans had all gone, we climbed back down through the trap door. Now we were alone. Just my mother and me in the dark, in a building that had been filled with our fellow Jews just an hour ago.

When morning came, we acted like nothing had happened. We went to work, just as we had before. The Germans apparently didn't correlate the names of the people they had taken away in the raids against the names of the people who were working every day. So long as we showed up for work, we continued to get our normal rations, meager as they were.

The Germans would never admit that they were taking people away to kill them. If you asked *Obersturmbannführer* Schwind, or any of the other Germans: "What happened to the people who were taken away?", you would always get the same response. "They're going to a better place. A place where they get better work, and better food." They would trot out the same cliché, the same mantra. *"Arbeit Macht Frei"*. "Work makes you free". They would tell us that if we made the commitment to work, they would give us the food. But no matter how hard we worked, the food never came. My father had been worked and starved to death. I don't know how much more committed you can be. But I guess, in a strange, sick way, he was free.

After a few days a new group of Jews, looking just as fat and healthy as we had six months before, moved into our room. We were packed in again, elbow to elbow. And then, after a few months, another nightmare came, another night-time raid. I pulled the same trick, hiding my mother and myself behind the tall rafter in the attic.

I felt wrong not to tell the others about our hiding place. But if I had told them, we all would have been caught. I still feel wrong about it, all these years later. I know I did it to save my mother, to save myself. I had no choice.

But it was an awful choice. On the one hand, we survived for a little while. I had beaten the Germans, outwitted the murderers, just a bit. I had a small, fleeting feeling of control. Those people who were taken away— well, just like before, nobody ever heard from them again. My mother and I were here. Alive. If only for another week. Another month. Maybe we could dodge another raid.

The people who had been taken just vanished from the face of the earth. We had no idea where they were being taken. We had been isolated, kept in the dark for years, most of us. We knew nothing of the outside world. What we did know was that once somebody was taken, they never came back. We lived in a vacuum, with no real word from the outside world.

My mother and I managed, through a little cunning and a lot of luck, to stay a few steps ahead of the raids and the roundups. It seems incredible now, but my mother and I survived in that purgatory for over three years, while waves of other people came and went. This was partly due to the fact that we both had, and managed to keep our jobs, which kept us out of danger at least some of the time. People were disappearing all the time. My mom's cousin Jacob, the one who worked with Schwind, the friend who had helped me get the job at the field, went home one day from work, and found that his entire family was gone. His block had been emptied. His wife and his three children had vanished into the air, scooped up in a daylight raid.

Erich Marx and his wife, Sharon, who worked in the farm office, both vanished in a raid one day. It was as if they had never been born.

One day in the summer of 1944, on August 16th, I received a notice that my mother and I were being assigned to help bring in the fall harvest. The notice promised that when we reported we would get a badge and papers that would qualify us for this big effort to bring in the crops that fall. It said that families could stay together and work together if they reported together. It promised that we wouldn't be separated, and that if we volunteered for this properly, we wouldn't be taken in any raid, day or night.

We were instructed to present ourselves in the courtyard between the German administrative barracks, near the ghetto office.

The way it had been presented to me, I was selected to be in this special harvesting group that was going to get this precious badge, a badge that would prevent us from being taken away to the camps in the East. And that if I hurried, I could bring my mom to get a badge too. Working at the field had been a real advantage for me, and I was anxious to help her get the same kind of work if I could.

I ran to get her. I convinced her that this was the right thing to do. When we arrived at the courtyard, however, things started to go wrong. First off, it seemed that there were too many people just to bring in a harvest. There must have been five or six hundred people, crammed in between these two buildings, lined up for these wonderful badges, whatever they might look like. I never found out.

It was a trap.

I'll always remember that the windows of the barracks were decorated with wooden Tyrolean shutters, the kind that can be closed over the windows on the outside to keep out the snow and wind. They gave the square the look of a place you would go for a winter vacation up in the Alps. I remember thinking that it was strange for those bright shutters to be closed during the day.

A shock and hush rolled through the crowd. The guards at the back started herding people forward. The head German officer at the end of the courtyard yelled: "*Achtung! Achtung!* Everyone on your feet! Everybody stand up!"

All the shutters flapped outwards, exposing the open windows. And behind every window were guards with machine guns, pointing out at us. There were dogs, barking out of the first–floor windows. Behind us was an open truck, now with a machine gun uncovered, cutting us off. We were caught like badgers in a cage.

From there, the joyride began.

Chapter 18

The Train.

The Germans herded us from the courtyard and into a narrow street. We didn't have far to walk. There was a railroad siding nearby, a heavily guarded station where they moved people and supplies in and out of Lodz—the place where we had come into the ghetto, months before.

There were six closed, rough box cars waiting for us. There must have been a couple hundred people trapped in there with us, squeezed into each rough wooden box. There wasn't a lot of commotion. What could we do? The Germans had us surrounded with dogs and guns and bayonets. Some of the people were moaning and complaining. Most of them were men begging to be allowed to go and get their wives and children, the families they had left behind when they were sent to the courtyard.

The train started chugging and rattling forward. The hot August sun beat on the roofs. And the heat of so much humanity, pressed into such a tight space, began to take its toll.

These were covered cargo cars, the kind used to move pigs and cattle to market. There were no windows, just some tiny openings up near the top that were covered with barbed wire. My mother and I were jammed in there together, pushed against each other, with no idea of where we were going, or what was going to become of us.

There wasn't room enough for any of us to lie down, or even sit down. So we jostled and elbowed each other. We took turns sitting or stretching out when we could get the chance. There were old men, old women, children, all jammed in there with the more able-bodied.

We had no food. No water. Just one dirty bucket, pushed in as the doors were closed and locked behind us, where we were supposed to pee, or to take a dump.

It was suffocatingly hot in the daytime. Some people just couldn't take it. A couple of older people died right there in the car. They just laid there, tangled under our feet, jammed in with the living.

The train rumbled on through the night, and into the next day. At one point in the afternoon the train stopped. We had no clue as to where we were, or what was happening to us. Because I was small and easy to lift, some of the older men hoisted me up so I could peer out through the wire, to see what was outside.

There was nothing. I couldn't see anything but fields. Just sky, stubble and soil. A few wires running on poles along the track, and that was it.

We sat there for what must have been a couple of hours. Then, as night began to fall, the train lurched forward again. The Germans did that on purpose, I believe, to wait until darkness to deliver us to our destination. Any time they were going to round us up, they liked to do it at night, so they could keep us shocked and terrified. Like animals being led to the slaughter.

The train screeched to a stop, and I heard shouting and banging. The doors were flung open, and we were blinded by spotlights aimed right in our eyes. "Get out," the Germans yelled. "Hurry now. Move! Move! Move!"

I was so terrified, my senses ground to a halt. All I could do was shuffle along with the rest. When you are that scared, exhausted and assaulted, your brain just tends to shut down, to go into survival mode. Which is what the Germans were counting on. I jumped out of the car, with people stacking up ahead of me and pushing behind me. The Germans were ready, prodding and beating us with guns, sticks and clubs if we showed any signs of hesitation, any hint of resistance. There were German Shepherds straining at their leashes, ready to rip us apart.

I turned and stopped for a moment, to help my mother down. She was weak from exhaustion and starvation, and very thin. She was 43 years old that night. But she looked old and helpless and weak, almost like a skeleton.

I tried to hold on to her, to help her any way I could. A couple of the other men and I got her onto the ground, our feet sliding and unsure on the sharp gravel, there by the long concrete train platform.

There were a lot of Germans, officers and SS, pushing us this way and that. They yelled and hit at the shuffling river of children, women and men. "Men to the right," they yelled. "Women to the left!"

I realized, just for an instant, that they were pulling my mother and me apart. They were ripping at us. It was like we were caught in a tornado and pulled into the sky, away from each other. There was a force to it, a whoosh that I felt. I remember the look on my mother's face, as if she was saying "What's happening? What can I do?"

I saw puzzlement and terror and confusion in her eyes. I'm sure she was seeing the same thing in me. I was 15, a young man, her child, her son. I was trying to take care of her. She was my mother—she was trying to take care of me. And neither of us could do a goddamned thing.

We had no chance to say goodbye. We were yanked apart, and that was it. It was like somebody had pulled my arm off. She was gone, dragged into the line with the other women.

Now I was alone in the flow of desperate men and boys and brutal, screaming Nazis. In the black night, with the spotlights in my eyes, I couldn't see. It was a maelstrom of scorching light and ink-black shadows. I could hardly see the people who were standing right next to me.

The guards forced our column, the men, down to the end of the platform. There was a high-ranking German SS officer there, resplendent in his uniform and peaked officer's hat, standing on an odd wooden box. He was scanning over the crowd, inspecting us as we were pushed near.

As each of us came up to him, in line, he flicked his riding stick one way or the other. He was splitting the men's column into two. He was sending what looked like older, weaker men and younger boys to the left. Taller, stronger men went to the right.

He looked at me, up and down, the way a butcher might appraise a steer. He pointed to the right.

Now, of course, people all over the world know what that meant. But for all I knew, he was just choosing which work detail I would be chosen for. Or which barrack I was going to sleep in.

We were force-marched into the night. We were pushed into a grey barrack where we were greeted by more German SS guards, and by other men in blue-and-white-striped uniforms.

The men asked if anybody in the group had been a policeman in the ghetto. Three guys raised their hands. It was, for them, a very bad idea. It looked like they hoped to get the same special treatment here, the extra food and privileges they had received in Lodz for working with the Nazis against their fellow Jews.

Instead, the Jewish men beat the hell out of them. They beat one of the ghetto policemen to death. His scalp was torn open, right in front of my feet.

"You have to take your clothes off," the SS men yelled German, which the inmates translated into Polish and Yiddish.

I stripped myself naked and threw my clothes on a pile with the others'. We were ordered to kneel down. I was shaking in fear. The men shaved our heads, the way a shepherd shears a sheep. Zip, zip, zip, and my mass of thick black hair was a clump, mixed with all the others' on the dirty floor.

They pushed me through a wooden archway that was spewing a harsh-smelling chemical from brass nozzles. They made sure we all got completely wet, that the stuff got under my arms and between my legs. The liquid hurt like hell. It burned like acid, especially where my scalp had just been shaved raw.

We were herded into a cold shower, 30 or 40 of us at a time. The ice-cold water sucked my breath away, but at least it got rid of that disinfectant, the poisons that were setting my skin on fire.

We were prodded out the other end of the building. At the exit, there was a mountain of clothing, and somebody in the shadows threw a uniform at each of us, a ball of rough, blue-and-white-striped cloth. There was a cap, a jacket and a pair of pants. Somebody threw a pair of shoes. Not in any particular size—just shoes.

We stood cold, naked and shell-shocked in a dark courtyard. We started trying to swap our clothes around to get something that actually fit us. I had shoes that were five sizes too big. So I looked around and found a guy with bigger feet and smaller shoes, and swapped with him. My jacket was so big, I looked like a clown. So I traded it for a smaller one.

One of the inmates said: "Welcome to Auschwitz". The first time I had ever heard that word.

I looked around, trying to get my bearings. We were surrounded by a brick wall on my left and a barbed-wire fence on my right, somewhere out there in the blackness.

As my eyes opened up to the darkness, I could see that the wall on my left was part of a building with an enormous smokestack. There were smoke and flames and sparks coming out of it, way above my head. And a choking, fat, sweet smell. A smell that seemed to ooze out of every brick and plank of wood in the buildings around me.

I remembered the other column of men marching alongside us from the train platform. The younger boys and the older, weaker men. The ones who had been sent to the left.

We were out here in the courtyard, trying on caps and trading shoes in the numbing night air. But the old men and boys who had gone into the other building, the one with the furious smokestack, did not come out at all.

Chapter 19

A raised hand. A tattooed arm.

It was cold and very dark. The sound of a whistle—the block elder's terrible whistle—seemed to stab me in the brain. The whistle dragged me down, like an anchor pulling a drowning man underwater, from my huddled sanctuary of sleep.

When I was dreaming, if even for a few moments, I could be myself again. Little Heinz Oster, the bright, curious kid from Cologne I used to be. I could sometimes remember what it felt like to be a human being— that restless, studious German boy who once had a life, a home, a family, a future.

But once I was awake, there was no me anymore. There was no place to hide.

The men around me rolled off their splintered wooden shelves and shook themselves into consciousness. I remembered the truth. That I was a Jew. A virus. A prisoner.

I remembered that my mother had been ripped away from me the night we arrived. I knew that she had surely gone to the gas chambers, and then the ovens, that first night in Auschwitz.

I remembered that I was freezing under my matted uniform. That I was aching, thirsty, hungry, and caked with dirt and sweat and my own filth. That my bones burned from tossing, with five other men, on a rough-hewn wooden rack. And that if I didn't drag my gaunt body into the courtyard fast enough, I wouldn't live to be pulled into the next of these black, hopeless mornings.

"*Appell! Appell!*" The barracks block elder, a German convict who had been promoted, through the insane logic of Birkenau, the death-factory subcamp of Auschwitz, to the stature of a minor god, shrieked the order to assemble. A current of prisoners shuffled toward the barrack door, streaming out into the frozen courtyard like cockroaches running from a torch. We were all terrified to be noticed as the slowest, loathe to be seen as the fastest, afraid to stand out in any way. In my first months here, clinging to life in this antechamber of death, I had learned that the only way to keep breathing was to be a ghost. My goal in life was to be invisible, forever unseen by the block elders, the collaborating Jewish kapos, and the pitiless SS guards.

If they couldn't see me, they couldn't select me. Being selected, we all knew, meant a one-way trip to the gas. And then being thrown into the ovens of the crematoria, whose smokestacks glowered like vultures over Birkenau, never truly out of sight or mind, burning and roaring just over the shingled barracks roofs.

The Germans, my countrymen and tormentors, took great pains to deceive us, to comfort us, to forestall panic among us prisoners. There were only a few of them, and thousands of us. They had the guns. But they knew we had the numbers. So they did everything they could to manipulate us into following their orders. They would say anything to forestall the animal terror of men, women and children when they knew, for sure, today, this second, that they were being herded to their deaths.

Despite their lies and their deceptions, we all knew. We didn't want to know. But we knew. We knew that the smoke and flame and ash that poured out of the smokestacks—the hellish smokestacks that towered over the complex—were the last earthly remains of our fellow Jews. They were the last traces of the older, weaker men, and of the women and children who arrived, day after day, in boxcar after boxcar, at the Birkenau railroad platform. The innocent people who had gone through the same selection I had, but who, at the whim of a German, at the flick of a swagger stick, had been sent the other way. The ones who, like my mother, had been sent to the left.

At 15, I was now a little tall for my age—which may well have been why I had been spared on the platform that first night. I was tall, but thin. My body had adapted to the meager rations, the never-ending fear, the restless sleep, the knotted struggle to stay alive. It was the only life I knew. I had mastered the craft of blending into the flow of despairing humanity around me. I kept my head down, never risking eye contact with a German, always keeping a more-visible prisoner between my thin form and the eyes of the SS.

This black morning, as every other morning for the past few weeks, we prisoners divided ourselves into rows of five, in the frozen mud and biting wind of the Polish winter. *"Appell"* was the twice-daily roll-call, and the SS guards conducted it with absurd Teutonic gravity. Not even death could spare you from the ordeal. Each prisoner had to be counted, dead or alive. If a prisoner had died in the barracks during the night, or in the primitive hospital, or off on some work detail elsewhere in the sprawling camp, or had flung himself against the electric wire, or hung himself in the latrine, the Germans demanded that the corpse be produced in the morning, held up by the luckless prisoner next to him, the body still holding its place in the ranks of the wretched and the doomed.

With painful deliberation, the block elder counted his charges. When he finished, after checking and rechecking, he reported his tally to the SS guard overseeing the barrack. The guard did his own checks and counterchecks—inspecting the prisoners, castigating the block elder, and making himself as self-important and unpleasant as possible. Then he, in turn, delivered his tally to his superior—who was very likely to institute his own checks and tallies, creating delay after excruciating delay.

Appell often took three or four hours—hours when we were forced to stand at attention, in the numbing cold or the bone-chilling rain, wearing nothing but the dirty uniforms of rough, indigo-striped cotton. On a good day, this was just torture. But in the rain, or biting wind, it was often fatal. Prisoners simply died where they stood.

If a prisoner fell out of ranks, or fainted, or attracted attention in any way, the guards beat the wretch with their pistols, their ever-present swagger sticks or their steel-toed boots. If the prisoner died from the beating, so much the better—the corpse was already in line, in place, ready to be counted.

This morning, *Appell* went by without too much drama and pain. We were released to shuffle back to the barracks, to start another day of doing nothing.

I was the only prisoner in my barrack who spoke German. Most of my barrack mates were Polish Jews who had little use for the slight, quiet teenager who spoke the language of their captors. I had no friend here, no advisor, no protector. Or even a God—I had given up praying and believing long ago. All I had in this world was my cup, my stained, baggy uniform and my own bony, underdeveloped body.

After the morning feeding of hard-crusted bread, the prisoners slowly spread out, wandering without purpose through the rows of wooden barracks. Other than forming up for *Appell*, jostling for food or dying, there was simply nothing else to do.

The Germans had spared us for the time being, for some perverse, unknowable purpose. I, and my supposedly useful fellow prisoners, didn't really live here at Auschwitz/Birkenau. We were stored here, like so many crates of cabbage, so many bales of hay. All we could do was wait. Wait for typhus, or starvation, or scarlet fever or pneumonia to take us. Wait to be beaten to death. Wait to be hung for some minor infraction. Wait to be selected, to be carted off in one of the sinister trucks. To disappear into the air, reduced to ashes and smoke.

Late in the morning, I drifted over to the latrine shed, walking with slow deliberation, saving every calorie of energy. I sat on the rough, cold board over the open trench of sewage, struggling to make something, anything come out. If you don't really eat, I had learned, you don't really defecate.

I had just managed to pass a hard, dense pellet when a prisoner stuck his head into the room. "They're making a selection!" he yelled. "They want teenagers. Just teenagers!"

I don't know why, but I found myself struggling to stand, gathering my pants around my tiny waist and running toward the courtyard. If you wanted to keep living, I knew, you never volunteered for anything. That was the conventional wisdom repeated, night after night, as we lay stacked like so many rolled-up rugs on the sleeping racks. But now, for a reason I didn't understand, I wanted to volunteer. It might have been the sheer monotony of waiting, decomposing, starving. Something, anything, must be better than this. Or at least an end to this.

The courtyard was already filling with a couple hundred teenaged boys like me, boys who had responded to the call, or who had been herded into the yard by their block elders. These were all the boys imprisoned in Birkenau—fewer than two hundred boys in a sea of older Jewish men. We were quickly arranged across the courtyard, twenty or twenty-five across, eight rows deep.

SS officers sorted the prisoners at the front of the crowd, pointing at some to move over to the left. Which way, if either, led to something better? There was no way to know, no time to think. Was this an opportunity, a chance to live? Or a gateway to death—just another in the Germans' endless series of bizarre deceptions? Stuck in a back row, I realized that I had little chance of being picked, for whatever this was.

I heard a small voice call out in German. I was startled to realize that the voice was my own. I found myself raising my hand to make myself seen from the back. *"Ich spreche Deutsch!"* I yelled, struggling to catch the eye of the selector. " I speak German!"

The German raised his chin, looked right at me and said, *"Du da!"* "You there!" He herded me from the back of the formation with his stick, the grim conductor of a desperate orchestra. "Over here," he barked, pointing the smaller group, over to the side, the ones he had selected before.

I looked around at my fellow selectees. This gave me a small measure of encouragement. My groupmates seemed to look a little stronger, a little sharper, a little less starved than the rest. And at Birkenau, the stronger you looked, the healthier you appeared, the longer you kept breathing.

The rejected boys, still locked in formation, had no idea whether they had missed the boat, whatever boat it might be. Or whether they had just been spared a horrible end. But many of them seemed to sense that something had passed them by.

Some grumbled. Some moaned. Some cried. We chosen boys were still unsure, still terrified. But we had at least been chosen. And in this courtyard, on this day in Birkenau, it somehow felt better to be chosen than to be left behind.

The guards marched us into a long barrack bordering the courtyard. As my eyes adjusted to the darkness, I made out a long line of tables, each manned by two German soldiers. The Germans had a record-keeping ledger opened at each table, along with a pen and inkwell, and a strange syringe filled with black fluid.

"This is not so bad," I thought, with a small spark of hope. "They're going to take my history, ask some questions, do some record-keeping. It's almost as if I'm worth something."

The SS officer in charge ordered us to line up in front of each table. And to roll up our left sleeves. As I reached the table, a guard ordered me to state my name. "Heinz Adolf Israel Oster," I said—the Germans had added "Israel" to the name of every Jewish male.

He entered my name in the record book. He gave me a stern look, and made an angry comment about my name—he didn't like the fact that it contained the words Adolf and Israel so close together.

Then the other German gripped my left hand and held it down with surprising force. The first German started jabbing the ink-filled hypodermic needle into my arm, etching a pattern of characters, dot by dot, into my shaking, bleeding forearm.

I realized that I was being tattooed. Through the blood and ink, I could make out my number—the big, slightly crooked number I can look down and see today on my arm—as I walked away from the desk. It was official. I was Heinz Adolf Oster no longer. I was now B-7648.

We boys were marched, wincing and bleeding, outside the barbed-wire compound. A row of slab-sided trucks awaited just outside. Guards ordered us, with their usual impatience, to climb up into the trucks. Our little convoy started rumbling, in line astern, to a destination unknown.

I found myself packed shoulder to shoulder in the vault-like truck body. Most trucks in my short experience were roughly constructed, with gaps and holes where light would streak in. But this truck had none. I saw strange felt gaskets around the door and window openings, as if the truck had been built to keep the outside air out—or the inside air in.

The boys crammed in with me were shocked, bleeding and bewildered. We commiserated back and forth in the darkness, speaking the Yiddish I had picked up in the Ghetto, as the trucks lurched slowly away from Birkenau. "Where are we going?" "Are they going to put us to work?" "Are they going to gas us all?" "Shoot us?"

Photo: U.S. Holocaust Memorial Museum Archive

Jewish women and children walking to the Birkenau gas chambers. This group,
from the Sub-Carpathian Rus region of Hungary (now part of Ukraine),
were selected for death at the Birkenau railway platform,
as was Henry Oster's mother, Elisabeth Haas Oster.

The convoy of trucks stopped, and there was a scraping, creaking sound overhead. I later saw that it was the rusted main gate of the Auschwitz main camp—the iconic arched gate with *"Arbeit Macht Frei"*— "Work Will Make You Free"—cast in black-iron letters, spread out in silhouette above the roadway.

Like sheep, we were herded out of the dark trucks to stand blinking in the harsh sunlight. So this was our new home: the brick buildings, curled concrete posts and barbed wire of Auschwitz I.

We were assigned to our two-story brick barracks, with the same rough, splintered-wood sleeping shelves as before. We were then left to stew for the rest of the day, to wander yet another bleak compound, to do nothing but worry, and wonder, and dread what the Germans had planned for us.

Chapter 20

To The Stables.

Well before the next dawn, our new block elder barked and herded us into the yard, just as the day before. The elder of this new barrack was another German criminal, one who had earned his place in Auschwitz by an act that shocked even the SS guards. He had murdered his mother, a crime held in especially low regard in German criminal culture, even by other hardened murderers, rapists, thugs and thieves.

We young ones, 131 new recruits in all, were separated from the others and ordered to fall into columns, four across. We were marched out through the barbed-wire gate, trotting in formation, the Germans, as always, harrying our ranks with their incessant yelling. "*Schnell, schnell, schnell,*" they barked, every time we moved. "Hurry. Hurry. Hurry." It seems a cliché now. In every World War II movie we see the Nazis with their German Shepherds, their swagger sticks, yelling *"schnell, mach schnell!"* at everyone. But it's a cliché based in fact. That was really how it was.

After half an hour of marching, through barbed-wire gates, through fields and administration buildings, we came to a another set of low wooden buildings that looked, from the outside, like painted versions of the wooden barracks we had left behind in Birkenau.

SS officers divided us into groups of ten or twelve, sending each group into one of the barracks. When we entered the buildings, expecting to see the usual rows of sleeping shelves, we instead found ourselves in real stables, with rows of stalls filled with snorting, sighing, panting horses. After all these days and nights of living in human misery, packed together with my fellow prisoners like rats, the warm smell of hay and horse urine and manure actually felt reassuring. It smelled rich. It smelled more like life than death.

I allowed myself a moment of relief, looking around at the horses, my fellow prisoners, and the Germans, who were acting just a bit less threatening than usual. "At least we are going to be put to work," I thought. "And they wouldn't bring us here, and go to the trouble of bringing us to the horses if they were just going to shoot us."

Two SS officers entered the barracks and started to explain, echoed by a Polish translator, exactly what we were to do and exactly how we were to do it.

There were 28 horses in the stable, and we learned that most of them were pregnant mares about to contribute their foals to the German war effort. Europe, especially Eastern Europe, was still largely a horse-drawn society, and the Germans needed every drop of gasoline for their tanks and trucks and the Luftwaffe's airplanes. It turned out that the railroad gauge—the space between the tracks, where the train cars had to fit—was wider in Russia than in Germany, so the German locomotives and cars were useless there until the tracks had been converted. Because of this, the Germans needed hundreds of thousands of draft horses to move men, weapons and supplies in all the occupied territories, and this complex of stables was just one of the hundreds they had set up to meet that demand.

Each of us boys was assigned three or four mares to care for. The Germans made it very clear that the horses were far more valuable than we prisoners were. If something happened to one of the horses in our care, or to its foal, we could be sure we wouldn't draw breath long enough to be assigned another. We would become what the Germans called the Sunday Entertainment, just as in the Lodz Ghetto: we would be hung at the main gate, at high noon, with the camp's military band providing its grim sound track.

Each of us was given a bucket, a grooming brush and a shovel. The officers showed us how we were expected to water the horses, to groom the horses, to feed the horses with hay and carrots and clover, and to carry away the horse manure and the urine-fouled straw. They also told us that stealing food from the horses—pocketing a carrot, or cramming some grain into your mouth when you thought nobody was looking— would also bring the death penalty. We believed them.

We were put to work, long, hard work, each of us tending his mares from before dawn to nearly midnight. The work was tough, but it was almost pleasing. I felt the blood start to move in me again—the exercise made me feel better than I had for a long time. It was far better to be doing something, anything, than to waste away, waiting to die back in Birkenau.

As we marched double-time through the dark that night, in rigid formation, back to our new sleeping barracks, I found myself feeling just an ember of hope. It was possible that I might live for a few more weeks, even a few more months, if I kept my eyes open, my head down, and did this precious job well.

Then the dread rushed back in. "The horses were well tended before we got there," I thought as I jogged, in formation with my fellow prisoners, through the cool Polish night. "Somebody had to have taken care of them before we came."

Something sudden, and decisive, and probably very bad, had happened to the previous caretakers. Could it be long before the same thing happened to me?

Chapter 21

Mutti, Olga and Barbarossa.

Our job at the stables quickly developed into a routine. After the pre-dawn morning roll call in front of our barracks in the main camp, we were marched, in two lines, about a mile out to the stables. And in the evening, after a 12-to-16-hour work day, we would be marched back, always after dark.

I was assigned two horses to take care of, two mares which were already pregnant with that season's foals when we—the 130 stable boys and I—were assigned to the Auschwitz stables. The Germans had named the mares before I got there. One was named Mutti, and the other was Olga; there were wooden signs with the mare's names carved into them, nailed over each stable door.

Most of the other boys had three or four mares to care for. But because I could speak German, I was also assigned to take care of the huge stallion, Barbarossa, which was there to be the stud for this harem of females. It was a much bigger job to take care of a stallion, because of the extra work involved with the mating process, so I wound up with just the two mares.

Barbarossa was a towering, beautiful, reddish-brown Arabian. To me, a skinny, starving city kid, he was absolutely gorgeous. Because he had been taught and trained in German, and only responded to commands in German, as the only German-speaking boy I was chosen to be his caretaker.

It was a huge responsibility, and I have to admit that it made me just a little proud to be chosen to take care of him. It also elevated my status among the other stable boys. Who were none too fond of me in the first place—I was the only German-speaking kid in the midst of all these Polish, Jewish boys. But because I could communicate better with the guards, it was a little easier for me to stay out of trouble. They tended to trust me a little more, I think.

It was my job to feed these three horses, walk them, wash them, groom them, and clean up after them—whatever they needed. And of course we had to maintain the stables: bringing in hay and carrots and oats and clover for the horses; shoveling and moving manure and dirty straw. We did it all. I was expected to learn how to help the mares through mating, through their pregnancies, and with helping them give birth.

We were there to do everything possible to keep these horses healthy, and to get them to produce as many foals as possible for the German war effort. We were just cogs in the machine, slaves to be used up and thrown away. But if we did our job well, we thought, there would be no good reason for the Germans to do away with us. Not that they ever needed a good reason, but the theory was that if we were helping the war effort, if we made ourselves difficult to replace, we might just stay alive.

We discovered that as we were feeding the horses, day in and day out, we could steal a little bit of the food now and then. We could hide a few oats, or some carrots, when the Germans weren't looking. We could also steal some milk from the mares after they had given birth. Sometimes the foals would get sick right after they were born. They got diarrhea, and when they did they would lose the urge to nurse from their mothers.

We would also, in secret, let the foals drink water instead of mare's milk, so the mares would have milk left over. When that happened, we could sneak a few mouthfuls of horse milk when the guards weren't paying attention.

If the Germans had caught us, it would have been all over. They staged inspections every day, where they would force us to open our mouths so they could look inside with a flashlight. If they found some chewed bits of carrot, or a pocket full of oats, you were done. We would be taken away and hanged the next Sunday, as simple as that. If we did eat a little something during the day, we made sure to wash out our mouths right away, to hide the evidence.

It's amazing what you can do if your life depends on it. It was worth risking your life today, because if you didn't get enough to eat—and we never did—you were going to starve in a few weeks anyway. The Germans would inspect our bodies and our clothes during the day. But they wouldn't check us at night when we were marched back to the barracks. We found ways to hide a few bits of food, here and there around the stables during the work day, and then come back and pick them up in the evening before we went back to camp.

It was important to never use the same hiding place two days in a row, because if the guards saw you going to the same corner too often, they'd figure out what you were up to. Today, a carrot goes over here, under a brick. Tomorrow, up under the eaves of a horse's stall.

I figured out a little hiding place of my own. The stall where I kept Barbarossa was also the place where we would wash the horses every few days. So there was a hole in the concrete, in the floor, for the water to drain. I used a nail to work the screws loose, so I could pull up the plate that covered the drain. I would sneak a couple carrots down there, and then at night, as we were finishing our work, I could get the carrots and sneak them in my clothing, and try to smuggle them into the barracks.

We made sure not to make any noise when we would slip something into our stomachs. One crunch of a carrot in the middle of the night, when we were marching back home, would be a death sentence.

I would also eat the clover they gave us for horse feed—you could hide it out of the way in the trough where the horses ate, so there would be a little left after the horse was finished. But I couldn't eat a lot of that—it was basically a competition between me and the horse. You can't eat the clover flowers. But the green clover leaves would give us just a little more nourishment, nourishment the others couldn't get. That's how we survived, myself and the other stable boys. We had just a little more access to bits of food here and there, a little extra energy to keep us going.

Chapter 22

The Foal In The Field.

My mares, Mutti and Olga, were pretty early in their pregnancies when I was assigned to the stables. Every day they got bigger and bigger.

Some days we would take the horses out into the fields nearby to let them graze, and allow them to get a little exercise. We were still enclosed within the huge Auschwitz compound, all fenced in with guard towers and barbed wire, so we never really imagined that we could escape. There was no place to escape to—no people, and no villages. I was in the middle of a strange country, ruled entirely by the Germans, so I was sure that nobody would help me or hide me, or feed me if I was foolish enough to give it a try. And it wasn't as if I could blend in to wartime Poland—I had a roughly shaved head, a tattooed arm, a striped uniform and a starved, skeletal body. To the Germans, I was a worthless Jew. To the Poles who lived here, I was even worse: A German *and* a Jew.

Being out in the fields gave me a little bit of freedom, though. And it let me pick some greens that I would find out in the pastures, or along the sides of the road.

I learned that dandelions, if they are picked at the right season of the year, could be edible, and give me a little more nourishment. The trick is to pick them before the flowers open up—they change, and get incredibly bitter after that.

There were some other weeds and plants that, through trial and error, I learned to pick and eat. I kept a tiny shard of steel in my pocket to pry up a plant or a root whenever I found one.

One day, late in the afternoon, I was out in a big field with my two mares when Olga fell over on the ground and started going into labor. I had thought Mutti would be the first to give birth because she was getting to be as big as a house. But no, it's Olga, and here I am, all alone in the field with these two mares, and one is flopping around on the ground about to foal.

We happened to be in a depression in the pasture, where they had planted clover where the water tended to pool. Then the four-o-clock siren went off, signaling that it was time to come in to the stables for the evening chores and roll call.

I'm in big trouble. Olga is giving birth, right here, right now, with stupid Mutti standing off to one side, completely oblivious. If I abandon Olga in the field now to make it in before roll call, and something happens to her or the foal, I'm dead. But if I stay here with her, the guards will take their count, find out that I'm missing, and sound the alarm. They will think that I'm trying to escape. And if they think there is an escape attempt, the whole camp will go crazy. I had seen it many times before. They will shoot first, and ask questions later. Or, more probably, not ask questions at all. After all, it's just a Jew. And a Jew in Auschwitz is going to die sooner or later. Why not sooner?

I decided to stay with Olga. She was my responsibility, and my friend, and I didn't want to leave her here alone. She was moaning and groaning, thrashing around in pain. I looked up into her birth canal, like I'd been taught, and sure enough, there were two little legs. Horses are supposed to come out with their forelegs first, and then their head tucked down in between, like a skier in a tuck position. So the legs were right, but the head was off to one side.

I had to reach inside the wet, bloody birth canal with my arm, find the head, and pull it around so it was pointed properly. If I didn't, Olga would die, the foal would die, and so would I, once the Germans found out.

It took a lot of strength, but fumbling around inside this poor horse's womb, I managed to pull the head of the foal around. The foal then slipped all the way out, and I held it so it would slip gently to the ground. It was covered with the slippery birth sac, like a clear raincoat, smeared with goo and amniotic fluid. And I could see right away that the foal was dead. It was bloated and lifeless. A lot of the foals had been coming out that way this year. There was an infection or something going through the stables at that time, which was causing a lot of miscarriages and stillbirths.

I stopped for a few seconds to get my breath. I could hear the uproar over the hill, coming from the camp. I could hear the guards yelling, I could hear the German Shepherds barking, and I knew that they were running around like chickens with their heads cut off, eager to shoot a runaway Jew. I peeked up over the hill, and I could see them coming. Six or seven soldiers were running, carrying their Mauser rifles, along with three or four dogs, all rushing up the slope.

I thought, "This is my last day. " I saw a branch on the ground, fallen from a nearby oak tree. I grabbed the branch and put my cap on it, my dirty grey- and blue- striped cap, and waved it up above the hill, so the soldiers could see it before they saw me.

Sure enough, one of those idiots shot at the cap—just reacting to anything moving. I started yelling, in German, "I'm here! I'm here!", waving my hat over my head.

They all came over the hill and saw me screaming, with the mare lying on the ground, and the dead little foal there with her. The guards were all pointing their rifles at me, yelling and screaming. Some of them were Ukrainians, not Germans, so they didn't all understand German well enough to know what I was saying. A lot of the guards and soldiers there were Ukrainians who had joined the Nazis, and if anything the Ukrainians were more cruel than the Germans. A German might hesitate before he shot you, he might think about it a second or two. The Ukrainians were like abused children who become bullies—they tended to be even more ruthless.

The leader, one of the Germans, decided to test me—to make sure I wasn't an escapee from another camp, I guess. He wanted to know my prisoner number. Not the one tattooed on my arm, but the number stitched onto my uniform, the uniform number they gave me when I first came into Birkenau. Even though it had been there on my chest since I arrived, I couldn't remember it. I had no idea. It just wasn't something anybody would normally ask me, so in my mortal panic I couldn't recall it.

I'm was sure I was going to die. I kept repeating, in German: "I'm not running away! I stayed here with the mare because she was giving birth! It's not my fault that the foal is dead!" A German-speaking Jew was very rare, at that time in Auschwitz. So that tended to make them sit up and listen a little. And they, perhaps, had a little more compassion for a German Jew than they would for a Polish Jew.

The leader took a breath. He seemed to believe me. "I might make it after all", I heard myself think. They left two soldiers with me. We waited until Olga could stand up again.

The dead little foal was still covered by the slimy grey membrane. The mare is supposed to bite and lick it off the foal, and to encourage that I was trained to sprinkle salt on the membrane, to entice the mare to start the process. I think horses eat the membrane and placenta to make sure that predators, like wolves, don't smell the placenta and the blood and come running whenever they smell a horse giving birth. If the mare doesn't eat the placenta, they sometimes get sick and vomit themselves. And it also helps the mare to recognize her foal, out in the herd with all the other foals. At least that's what we were taught in the stables. Out here in the field, though, surrounded by soldiers, I didn't have any salt.

But Olga was a good mare and she did it instinctively, all by herself. Even though her foal was dead, Olga struggled to her feet and licked it clean. The soldiers that had gone back to camp sent out a small horsedrawn cart, and they hoisted the little foal onto the cart to take it back to the stables. So I finally brought my two mares home, back inside the stalls, not knowing whether I was out of the woods or not.

One thing that might have saved me was the SS veterinary assistant who inspected the dead foal. He couldn't be seen showing any kindness or weakness to a Jew, so he yelled at me, at the top of his lungs, that the foal's death wasn't my fault—*"Es ist nicht deine Schuld!"* In this way he could get his message across to the other Germans and Ukrainians there in the camp, and still not appear to be doing me any favors.

Once the head count was done the head of the stables took my head off anyway. But only figuratively. The precious head count had been delayed here, so his report would get to headquarters late, and the whole crazy Teutonic universe had been disturbed. I had done the only thing I could but of course that didn't matter. He looked at the dead foal. He called me a dumb Jew. He ranted and raved. And of course all my fellow stable boys were standing out there waiting. Nobody could go back to camp until every single head was counted.

Finally, well past midnight, he let us march back to the barracks. We would be up at 4 the next morning, just like every other day, to march back out again.

Chapter 23

Barbarossa.

Horses have a ritual they go through when they mate. The stallion doesn't just get an erection any time he wants. It's a process the two horses go through to make it all happen—kind of like dating and foreplay in humans, but on a much bigger, more-primitive, more-violent scale.

It doesn't always work out the way it's supposed to. The horses are upset by having humans around. At the same time, they are excited, and kind of frantic, so sometimes they need a little help to make everything come out right. This complex of stables was an assembly line of horses, after all, and the Germans didn't want to waste time with a mating that didn't produce a pregnant mare.

It was my job as Barbarossa's keeper to help the process along in any way I could. This was big entertainment for the German officers, who would gather whenever a breeding session was scheduled. It was a great spectator sport for these guys, watching this skinny Jew from Cologne caught between this rearing, snorting stallion and a panicked, kicking mare.

The horses didn't think it was funny at all. And I wasn't laughing. I was just trying to not get myself killed.

Barbarossa, like any stallion, would go through a sequence of nuzzling the mare, nipping at her neck, and making this purring, vibrating sound in his throat, which horse breeders call nickering. He would sniff and snort at her, and if everything was going well, he would get an erection. A really gargantuan erection. An erection the size of a lake trout. If she was in the mood, she would raise her rump, lift her tail and try to help things along. This was all happening inside a confined stall, to help keep her in place in case she changed her mind half the way through. So there's a big mare and this towering stallion—about 3000 pounds of frantic, horny horses. And little me, flailing around on straw in this rough wooden box.

I would lead Barbarossa into the stall and pull his head toward the mare, encouraging him to start the process. This would all take place when the mare was in estrus, a period of a few days when she's ready to conceive, the short time when she is sexually interested in the stallion. Or at least that was the theory. In practice, she may or may not be all that interested, and Barbarossa doesn't really enjoy having me or all these laughing, yelling Germans around when he's trying to concentrate on mating with this nice young mare.

It was also my job to guide the stallion's member into the mare, if he was having trouble doing it himself. So I'd be darting around, terrified, wrestling with this monstrous horse penis, trying to help him find where to put it.

He didn't like this one bit. So he would be pawing at me with his forelegs, shoving me aside, biting at me, hitting me on the hands with his hooves—sometimes cutting my hands up pretty badly.

Even the horse's tails were dangerous. Horsehair is rough and abrasive—that's why it works in the bow of a violin, because it grabs the strings and vibrates them. So my face and hands would be a mass of tiny cuts and scrapes every time I had to get in there between them.

At Auschwitz having any kind of cut or wound could mean death. Not just from the wound itself, or possible infection. It was because when the Germans saw a wounded Jew, they were likely to send that poor slob right back to Birkenau and into the gas chambers. The Germans were always staging inspections to select the weaker, sicker prisoners and send them up the chimneys.

At one point during a mating session I remember tripping and falling between Barbarossa's hind legs. I got caught under this massive, heaving stallion, getting kicked and trampled as I scrambled around, trying to not get squashed underfoot. And of course he was going nuts, rearing up and pawing at me, almost as frightened as I was.

His huge member was waving around like an elephant's trunk. The Germans standing around thought this was the funniest thing. They were cheering at me like I was the main attraction in a freak show: "Do it again!" they yelled. "Do it again!"

Chapter 24

In the line of fire.

In all the years since I was imprisoned in Auschwitz, there was one story I never talked about. There was one experience I never shared with anyone else.

It had never seemed to make sense to mention it to my family or my friends, or in the presentations I've given over the years at the Los Angeles Museum of Tolerance about my experiences in the Holocaust.

I guess because it was too hard to talk about, too hard to think about.

If I talked about something like this with a friend, or a family member, it always seemed like it would stop any conversation in its tracks. And I was hesitant to burden anyone else with it. What were they going to do? What could they say? If I thought about mentioning it at a presentation, I was afraid I would break down, and that I wouldn't be able to continue if I did. That didn't sound like all that much fun either.

So, it has been something that I have held inside all these decades. All my adult life.

The Germans in Auschwitz were obsessed with the fear of somebody escaping. Just the hint that somebody might beat their little system, that somebody might get out of there and tell the world what was going on, would drive them crazy. If there was an escape attempt or, even worse, a successful escape, they would respond with brutal retaliation. This wasn't exclusive to Auschwitz or the concentration camp system. The Nazis used reprisals—the retaliatory murder of innocent people—as a weapon throughout the entire war, as a way of instilling terror into the civilian population.

Any attack against the Germans, any sign of resistance, could result in tens, sometimes hundreds of civilians being slaughtered. As they did in occupied countries all throughout Europe, the Nazis would randomly gather innocent civilians and murder them without cause or trial, often in city squares, right in front of their neighbors, their wives or their children.

In Auschwitz, as you can imagine, the Nazi's brutality had almost no limits. In their own hellish world, cut off from the rest of civilization, they could get away with anything they wanted. And when there was any sign of rebellion or resistance, they did not hesitate in exacting revenge.

Trying to survive in a world like this was not just a physical problem. It wasn't just about keeping your body going. You also had to keep your mind going as well. In a crazy world, it's almost impossible not to go crazy yourself. And many prisoners did. Almost every night we would hear shots out by the wire. Inmates would give up and decide to kill themselves, by making a last dash out to the electric fences. And the Germans were more than happy to help them, shooting from the guard towers.

Our work at the stables had insulated us from much of this horror, at least for a few months. And the fact that we were boys, not men, may have helped us get through some of the horrors we saw and heard about, without losing our minds completely. But one night, out of the blue, I came face to face with what the Nazis were capable of.

It was a Saturday night. We were coming back into the camp from the stables, and I was at the back of the line of prisoners. Because I had to do the extra work with the stallion, I had been the last boy to finish up and lock the barn before we were marched back to the main camp, in our usual rows of four across.

As we stumbled through the darkness, I noticed that there was something strange happening at the main gate. On some Saturday nights in the past, if we had been allowed off work a little early, we had been led into a hall where the camp orchestra gave musical performances to entertain German prisoners.

So at first I thought that we were being sent to some kind of awkward entertainment.

There was a lot of commotion at the gate. There was a group of German soldiers there and a couple of trucks, more than just the usual Kapos and guards. I began to realize that this was no musical recital we were heading for. I thought to myself, "Uh oh, Heinz. Watch out. You are walking right into a selection."

As we marched in through the main gate, two German officers stepped forward and cut off the last row of our column. They shoved us, the last 4 stable boys, into a group of other men, mostly older than we were, who had been selected beforehand from other barracks. There was no reason given, no explanation. They just pushed us into this bigger group of men, like they were herding goats.

The Germans turned us to the left after the first building and then to the left again, past a couple of trucks and into the courtyard between two three-story brick barracks. There was a wall that closed off the courtyard at the back. I remember that the building on the left of this courtyard was the camp brothel, where some of the more attractive Jewish women were forced to have sex with some of the more-privileged German inmates and block elders.

We wound up against the wall, waiting there in the middle of the night, not knowing whether we were about to live or about to die. I remember it was very cold. We had no idea of what was about to happen. But we knew it probably wasn't going to be good.

There was a rustle of cloth, and a gasp and cry ran through the prisoners. I looked up and saw that the rear canvas curtains of the trucks at the front of the courtyard had been lifted up all of a sudden, and two machine gun crews that had been concealed in the trucks started firing, their muzzles flashing in the darkness, spitting bullets right into the crowd of prisoners. Right at me.

The moment we heard the machine gun fire, our first instinct was to fall down, away from the sound, to duck and try to get out of the way of the explosions and the bullets.

Because we had been the last group to be selected, we were at the back. I had a fairly tall guy in front of me who was hit in the first blast from the guns.

He fell back on top of me, and I felt a pain in my knee, and then I was under a pile of thrashing, heaving, dying men. There were so many people, packed in so tightly when the shooting started, that the gunners didn't have a clear shot to get the people at the back. We were also small, just boys compared to the other men, so the machine gunners had been forced to aim down at us from the height of the truck bed, and so they missed some of us in the confusion.

The machine gun fire stopped, but there were wounded prisoners screaming and moaning and scrambling on the ground, away from the bullets, trying to do anything to survive. I was able to peer over the shoulder of the body just ahead of me, and I could see that there were two German officers now, with their pistols out, going through the pile of dead and dying men. They were going one by one, shooting the wounded lying helpless on the ground in the backs of their heads.

My friends from the stables had also survived the first wave of bullets. We were stranded in a little pocket in the back, surrounded by the dead and dying, where the bullets hadn't reached.

There was a door not too far away, a door in the next building on the edge of the courtyard that led through a hallway that ran through the building. I whispered to my friends that we should all run together, to see if we could make it to the door. If we went one by one, they would have had a clear shot at each of us. But if we all went together—and remember, we were pretty small—we might have a chance. We were surrounded by blood, and bits of bodies, and death. It was the only chance we had.

I whispered the signal. "Now!" We scrambled up in one rush and raced for the open door—it was only a few steps away. I forgot the pain in my knee in the adrenaline and panic of the moment. In the chaos, with the Germans busy shooting people at the front, we made it across the courtyard and ran into the building.

We kept right on running, down the length of the building and out the door at the end. By sprinting from barracks to barracks, dodging the German guards when we had to bridge the short gaps, we managed to make it back to our own block.

If the Germans had seen that we had escaped from the courtyard, we were sure that they would finish us off. I've never been more terrified in my life. I had to struggle to control my breathing when I finally got to our barrack. I found that I had soiled my pants in my terror—I was a real mess.

I was not wounded very badly. It was more of a gash, a grazing wound, than a bullet hole. I could hide it from the block elder and the other boys. When I was alone, I made sure to clean the blood and poo from my clothing, and to mend the hole in my pants leg, so the Germans wouldn't see it and realize that I had been one of the few prisoners who had escaped the massacre. In all the confusion, mixed in with all those thousands of prisoners, I managed to get away with it. If I had been hit a little worse, if I had failed to make it to work the next day, or the next day after that, they would have found me out.

What do you do to treat a gunshot wound if you have no bandages, no doctor, no medicine? You urinate on it, to disinfect it the best you can. If it gets infected, you cover it with snot. You take it right from your nose, which is always running in the cold, and you use it as a protective film, and a kind of antibiotic.

If I had not been terrified before, I certainly was then. I was shattered to remember what we had been through, to know that we had been selected to die, that we had been machine gunned, and that for no real reason we could understand, we had survived.

The other kids in my group of stable boys who had been selected to be shot also made it out of the courtyard and back to the barrack. Maybe the German gunners were a little hesitant to shoot at boys, rather than men. Or maybe they missed because we were small, and hard to see in the dark, at the back of the condemned group.

Photo: Wikimedia Commons

The main gate of Auschwitz I, where Henry Oster
was selected to face a machine-gun firing squad in reprisal
for an escape attempt by Polish prisoners.

The Germans didn't make a big search of the camp to find us, which gave us a chance to slip back into our barracks before anybody knew we were missing. And of course we didn't say a word to anybody else about what had happened. That's one of the reasons that I'm unsure about exactly who had been targeted. We couldn't afford the luxury of talking about it to the other inmates, the ones who had been at the head of the line from work, and who didn't know about the shooting. We couldn't trust anyone. People would turn each other in, betray each other, send each other to the gas for half a slice of bread. Sometimes people would be suffocated as they slept, so another inmate could steal a crust.

I remember that one of the boys, the one right behind me in the courtyard, was hit in the foot. One was hit in the shoulder, and one in the side. But by some wild chance, none of us were killed that night.

It turned out that this massacre was a retaliation for an escape of 4 Polish Gentile prisoners that had happened that day, a brilliant escape that had help from the outside, from the Polish Resistance, and from inside the camp. To exact their revenge and to discourage anybody else from escaping, the Germans had the block elders select two prisoners from each barrack, to make sure everybody in the camp knew somebody who was killed.

In reprisal for the four prisoners who had escaped, the Germans decided to kill 43 prisoners—roughly ten for every escapee.

They wanted to spread the terror equally. But apparently the numbers came up short. The Germans needed a few more Jews to kill, and we boys had been in the wrong place at the wrong time.

Throughout the camp, that massacre came to be known by the Germans as the Saturday Night Theater. It was part of their sick sense of irony—like murdering Jews was their form of entertainment, somewhere between watching a soccer match and going to the opera.

Of all the things that happened to me, this was the one that shook me up the most. The only way for me to keep going, I guess, was to wall it off in my mind. To make believe that it hadn't happened. Or that if it did happen, it happened to somebody else. For the next 65 years, I did just that. My life had depended on my keeping this a secret. And that's just what I had done.

The next morning, Sunday, we were herded out, just as on many other Sundays, to the camp gallows. A German military band was set up, there, right next to the wooden platform. Three of the prisoners who had escaped had been trapped between the rings of barbed-wire fences and recaptured. They were executed there in front of us the next day, with the camp orchestra playing during their hangings. Like it was some kind of damned parade.

The Germans left two of them hanging there for two days.

They also left the bodies of the men who had been shot—the victims of the massacre that we had escaped—lying between the two buildings.

When we marched back and forth to work for the next couple days we were forced to go past the piles of bloody, machine-gunned corpses in the courtyard. And then the two hanged men at the gate, still twisting in the cold air.

Chapter 25

A beating, a tomato and a loaf of bread.

I was soon given another job as the runner for the stables. Just as in the Lodz ghetto, I had to deliver the reports back to the administration building every day. Because I had just three horses to take care of, the Germans had decided that I had the extra time to do this extra chore. And because I spoke German, there was likely to be less trouble with me getting through the camp. If a German challenged me or wanted to know what I was doing, I could tell him in his own language, which gave me a little leeway to move about between the stables and the administrative buildings.

On the way, every day, I had to pass a place called "Kanada". This was a small warehouse, near the main gate, where the belongings of the incoming inmates, dead or alive, were collected, sorted, and sent out to help the German war effort. Or what was left of the belongings, after the Germans and, to a lesser extent, the inmates who worked in Kanada, had stolen whatever they could get away with.

I didn't know this at the time, but it was known as Kanada (the German spelling) because the country of Canada was, from the perspective of Auschwitz, a fantasy land, a Shangri-La. To older, more worldly inmates who knew more about the outside world than I did, Canada promised to be most fabulous place on earth: free, clean, safe. And no Nazis.

There was a larger version of this sorting place in the Birkenau camp where I had first been imprisoned. The smaller warehouse, within the wire of Auschwitz I, was dedicated, I believe, to packaging and sending out specific products—clothes, hair, shoes, glasses, money, jewelry, watches, even extracted gold teeth—back into Germany, or to the various war factories within the Auschwitz complex.

Having a job in Kanada was as close as a Jew in Auschwitz could get to being secure and well fed.

The workers there were mostly women. At about 10:00 every morning I would walk by, and I could see the same women prisoners through the fence, sorting though the belongings of each new shipment of prisoners. I would wave and say hello, and we would talk a little bit. The women asked me where I was from, ask about any family that I might have. I remember they asked about my mother's name—on the slim chance that she was still alive.

And as we talked, every now and then one of the women would flip a piece of moldy bread, or some other morsel of food they had found in a new prisoner's clothes or luggage, over the fence for me. It was like they were feeding a pigeon.

Sometimes a woman would leave a bit of bread by the fence, as if it had fallen there. When nobody was looking, I could stoop down and grab it. If she had been caught, she would be in huge trouble. She had been selected to have this wonderful job, and now she was stealing food and giving it to other inmates?

Sometimes the prettier women who came into the camp were selected to work as prostitutes—as I mentioned before, Auschwitz had its own bordello, in the building to the left as you walked in through the main gate. These women—the prettier, sexier ones—would be taken aside when they arrived and offered a horrible choice: go into the general population, where they would probably be starved and worked to death, or become a prostitute for some of the more privileged inmates, usually guards and German nationals who were there because they had committed some kind of crime. These inmates would get a voucher if they were to be rewarded—a ticket good for a few minutes with one of these slave prostitutes. It was against the law for a German soldier to have sex with a Jew, but we knew that some of them patronized the bordello anyway.

The Germans gathered the more-attractive women together and spelled it out for them. If you do what we want, have sex with these soldiers and privileged inmates, you can have it really good here. You can stay here and be safe, and well-fed.

If a woman refused, if she protested, the Germans had devised a horrible punishment.

One woman who put up a struggle was set on fire, we had heard. When she had refused the Germans, one forced her legs apart, poured gasoline on her vagina and lit a match. Everybody knew about things like that happening—it got around the camp instantly.

The Germans called a woman's vagina a *Pflaume* or "plum", as part of their crude slang. And this incident became known as the *Pflaume Feur*—lighting the plum. If a woman was castigated by the other prisoners about her having sex with the Germans, she would say "I only do it because I have to. I don't want a flaming belly—a *Pflaume Feur.*"

The women who were forced to be prostitutes did get extra food, so they would be healthy and well fed for their customers. And if they had a passing acquaintance, or even a lover, they might lower a basket of food from their window.

The women back in the larger Kanada, in Birkenau, were given more menial jobs, like sorting the gold teeth that the men pulled from the corpses. Or sorting the hair that was cut when anybody arrived—the Germans used that as insulation on submarines, of all things. Most of the inmates' belongings were sent back to Germany, to help supply the folks at home during the war. They even used the bodies of some of the people who were gassed, or who died of starvation or disease. The fat was rendered to make soap. The bones were ground up to make calcium supplements for fertilizer, we found out later.

As I said, every now and then, through the kindness of the women in the Auschwitz I Kanada, I would get a moldy crust of bread. I've probably eaten more mold in my lifetime, more penicillin, than anyone alive. I would eat it while I was walking, just a few crumbs at a time. I couldn't save it or take it back to the barracks, because then I would have to share it with everybody.

I remember one friend who asked me if I could get him some food from Kanada. I did what I could—I shared some bread with him, in secret, whenever I could. His name was Josh—we called him Joshy, because he was just a kid like me.

I have no idea what happened to him. Whether he lived or died.

One time I tried to hide a piece of bread out in the camp, because I wouldn't eat the whole piece the first day. Because I had been starving so long, my system could only take small portions at a time. I went back the next day to get the piece of bread I had hidden near a tree. There was a German guard there, walking his German Shepherd. And the dog lifted his leg and peed right on the tree. Right where I had buried my bread.

I tried to wash it off, but I couldn't get the dog urine out of it. I was heartbroken. When you have nothing, the tiniest thing is a treasure. For that piece of bread, I would have given just about anything. And now it was gone.

I also had to pass by the camp bakery every day. The smell of the baking bread was agonizing and irresistible. I looked forward to it—it was something that at least smelled like food, like life, life the way things had been before Lodz and Auschwitz.

It was an exquisite torture to have that smell of flour and yeast and heat fill my nostrils, permeate into my brain, tease my watering mouth, and not be able to grasp it, to devour it.

There were privileged German inmates loading the bread from the loading dock into trucks every day, for distribution throughout the camp. So to add to my misery, I had to witness the loaves of bread being carried, stacked and loaded.

One day as I was walking past, trying not to look at the wondrous bread, a loaf dropped off the loading dock onto the ground. My hopes rose and then fell, as the inmate who had dropped it walked down the steps, picked it up and put it back on the truck. Over the next couple weeks, the same thing happened three times. I began to wonder why it was always dropping right when I walked past, at 10:00 AM.

I decided that maybe somebody on the bakery detail was dropping the bread on purpose. The next time I walked past I noticed this guy, probably a German national, a Gentile inmate, looking around, with his hand ready to knock the bread off the truck. Once he was sure the coast was clear, sure enough, he pushed it over and it fell.

It was an incredible risk. If I was caught stealing a loaf of bread, I would probably die. But hunger will make you do just about anything. I actually had the guts to scoot over, pick up the bread, and then start walking away as if nothing had happened.

I got about five steps before all hell broke loose. The man in charge of the bakery, an SS guy in a black uniform, started yelling at his workers to grab me for stealing. Before I had a chance to even smell the bread, they were dragging me into the bakery. The German officer screamed at me, and beat me with his swagger stick. He had the fancy uniform, the boots, the whole thing. He was a big man on campus—some German officer who had screwed up somehow, and now was in charge of this miserable bakery.

I begged him, yelling in German: "Please, please don't hit me!" I told him I was sorry. That I'd never do it again. A torrent of desperate German poured out of my mouth—I said anything I could think of, in sheer panic, to convince him to let me go, to let me live.

He stopped yelling. "You speak German," he said. "How come you speak such good German? You speak it very well."

"I'm a German." I said. 'A German Jew."

He was obviously surprised that a German teenager, even a Jew, could be here in Auschwitz, where almost all the other prisoners were older Polish men. I told him my story, that I had been here sent to Auschwitz from Lodz. He asked me, "Where in Germany do you come from?"

"I'm from Cologne," I said. He raised his stick again. I recoiled, raising my arm, expecting to get another smack on the head. But he hit his boot instead.

"Well damn it, that's where I'm from," he replied in amazement.

He chewed me out some more, as if it was his duty—as if he thought somebody might be watching. "How can you do such a terrible thing, stealing from the Reich? Don't you know what could have happened to you?"

I was shocked and shaking. Is he going to turn me in, send me to the gallows? Or will this evil-looking SS man, in his big hat and jackboots and black leather, actually spare my life?

He seemed to decide something. "You've had your punishment, Mr. Heinz Oster from Cologne. I'm going to let you go. So get out of here, and never let me catch you doing anything like this again, or it will be the last time you do anything."

He picked me up like a scarecrow, pushed me to the door, and kicked me out into the yard with his big boot, sending me tumbling from the concrete platform to the damp earth. My head hurt. I thought he had hit me again on the way out the door. Then I realized that there was a loaf of bread next to me, that he had thrown out with me.

I reached up to feel my head, and my hand came back red and wet. I thought I was bleeding. Then I saw that he had followed the bread with a flying tomato, a big ripe tomato that I had seen on his desk. He turned in the doorway and walked inside, leaving me on the ground with a loaf of bread and a tomato. It was like winning the lottery. It was better than that.

I ate the tomato and hid the bread, so I could come back each day and have a little more, to make it last. I even shared some of it with a friend of mine, the two of us nibbling at a piece of bread for the next ten days or so, crumb by crumb. In my entire time in Auschwitz, that was one of the few humane things a German ever did for me. A beating, a tomato and a loaf of bread.

Chapter 26

The Gauntlet and the One-Eyed Nazi.

My job as a runner gave me some freedom to find food, but it sometimes led me into situations that scared me out of my mind. In Auschwitz you could fool yourself into feeling that you were relatively safe one minute, and the next minute you'd be dead. So I never knew what I might be stumbling into.

Every 20 days or so we were given a shower in a special barrack adjacent to the camp's main latrine. After work, long after dark, we stable boys were marched in and ordered to take off our clothes. The Nazis were constantly looking for signs of weakness. There were always more people coming in to Auschwitz. To make room, people already there had to die. This was the end of the line. If you looked hurt or sick or more starved than the others, you would be selected for death.

The vultures of the SS took the opportunity to inspect their prisoners at these occasional showers. We were already undressed and lined up, so it was a perfect opportunity for them to check our scrawny bodies, to see if we had any wounds or signs of disease, to determine whether we could go on for a few more weeks of slave labor. Or whether we were used up, expired—not worth feeding for another day. We had heard through the camp grapevine what these selections meant. If you got a shower, you were OK. If not—well, that was your tough luck.

Prisoners who didn't pass would be pulled out of the shower line, forced to put their clothes back on, and held apart in the barrack. In the morning those poor unwashed Jews would be trucked to the Birkenau gas chambers.

For some reason we stable boys seemed to be immune to being selected. There may have been some order given, by some anonymous Nazi, that we were not to be singled out and murdered. We never really knew why, but our group of 131 boys was always waved straight through to the showers.

This was fortunate for us, but the experience was heart-rending. We could not avoid passing the mass of men who had been pulled out of line before we had arrived. They would be held under guard overnight, to prevent them from finding a place to hide, or escaping into the camp and telling the other prisoners about their fate. Once the Nazis had them, they never let them go.

Imagine looking into the face of man—a man who has done nothing wrong—who has just realized that this would be his last night alive. Now multiply that by 100 or more—the number of doomed, desperate Jews who were already singled out when we filed past, stark naked, to take our showers. Because we came back to camp later than everyone else, we would be forced to walk past nearly every prisoner who had been selected to die the next morning. Some seemed resigned. Some acted angry. Some—most of them—just looked shocked and horrified. I can never forget their faces.

I was amazed every time we stable boys walked out of that damned shower building alive. I felt an overwhelming flood of emotions: survivor's relief and survivor's guilt. As we stumbled toward our own barrack, cold and wet in the night, I could hear the cries and moans of the men behind us.

I knew that we had been lucky, very lucky, yet again. But in Auschwitz, we all knew, your luck could run out in a heartbeat. One morning, it very nearly did.

My job required me to make my way back to the main Auschwitz gate every morning with the daily reports. If we had taken a shower the night before, by the time I arrived, at about nine or ten AM, the doomed men would usually be gone, never to be heard of again.

This time there had been some delay, a broken cog in the machine of death. Rows of tall, canvas-covered stakebed trucks, 5 on the left and 3 on the right, were parked along the road just outside the gate. They were filled with the same wailing, desperate men I had shuffled past the night before.

The hair on my neck stood up, chilled with sweat. This was a very dangerous place for a lone Jew to be. If an SS guard spotted me in the middle of this chaos he might assume that I was one of the condemned men trying to escape, and force me on to one of the trucks. Or simply raise his Mauser and shoot me.

The only thing that distinguished me from the prisoners on the trucks was the sheaf of stable reports in my trembling hands. If a guard challenged me I might be able to use them to prove that I was here on a legitimate errand, and not one of the selected men. If he bothered to ask. The SS tended to kill first, and ask questions later.

I took one last breath and forced myself to walk down the middle of the road, eyes straight ahead, my papers held out in front like a shield, as if the trucks and men on either side didn't exist. I tried to close my ears and my brain, but I could hear the men calling to me. They cried out their names and their home towns, so their lives and deaths might be remembered. They begged me to tell their families what was about to happen to them, as if they were already dead. As if I could remember them all. As if I could do something to help them.

I could not afford to stop, or to say a word to these poor souls. If I wanted to live, I had to ignore them. I tried to look important, which was not easy for a 15-year-old Jew in Auschwitz. When I reached the door of the administration building, my breath coming in gasps, I felt as if I had run away from my own funeral.

As I did every work day, I handed my reports to the same SS officer in the administration building. He had told me he been wounded on the Russian front, and instead of being sent home to recover he had been kept in the SS and assigned to this hellhole. He had just one eye left, and his face had been destroyed by Russian shrapnel. It was red and molten, like raw hamburger straight from the meat grinder.

His face was hideous, but underneath it all he showed signs of being a decent human being. We had talked a bit in the previous weeks, as part of our daily routine, and he had told me that even though he had no choice in the matter—he was, after all, an SS officer—he was opposed to the wholesale murder that was going on in the camp.

The trucks were still out there, and even inside the building I could hear the wailing. I tried to hang around inside as long as I could. I had no intention of going back out one second before I had to—I was hoping the trucks would move along on their grim journey, so I would be safe from being forced onto one of them. I knew that my sheaf of papers had saved me coming in, because they gave me an air of purpose and authority. But if I walked back without the papers, through that corridor of death, it would look like I was running away. Just what an escapee would do.

The maimed officer noticed that I was lingering longer than usual. "Get out of here," he barked.

I pointed out toward the mob scene outside the gate. "How do I know the guards will not shoot me when I walk through?" I asked him, my voice shaking.

He peered out the window with his one eye. "I see." He stood up and walked toward the door. "You don't need to worry," he said. "I'll walk out there with you."

We must have made an odd couple, walking through the iron gate and up that graveyard of a road—a ghost-pale Jewish teenager and a mutilated SS officer. He walked with me past the trucks, then turned back while I went on up the road.

I was so frightened I peed myself. When I got back to the stables, I had to hang my pants up to dry.

Chapter 27

Something's Happening Here.

In the winter of 1944, in late November, things began to change for us. The Germans took us stable boys away from the Auschwitz main camp, away from the horses, and transported us into a brand-new sub-camp called Plawy, a few hundred yards to the west. I've never found out what Plawy was designed for, or who was supposed to be kept there. For us, it merely served as a holding camp, another place where the Germans stored us while they decided our fate.

One Sunday, instead of going back to the main camp after work, we were taken to this strange new place. It was pristine and clean, like nothing we had seen in Auschwitz before. But things didn't seem right. We were taken out of a camp and a work situation that was relatively safe, a situation we had gotten used to. It had been our home. Now, like everything else, it was gone.

The Germans just plunked us there with nothing to do for about a month. The Germans seemed to be acting more strangely every day. There was something in the air—they were not acting with their usual arrogance and air of authority. There was an undercurrent of fear, of uncertainty.

We had no idea of what was going on in the outside world. We had no idea of how the war was going, whether the Germans were winning or losing. But later we found out that what had the Germans so spooked was the Russian Red Army, roaring in from the east, gobbling up Poland and heading right for Auschwitz. Now the Nazi supermen were about to be hunted down, defeated, probably killed or captured and turned into slaves themselves.

The Germans had treated the Russian people horribly. They had destroyed most of Western Russia, exterminated Russian Jews, raped Russian women and tortured Russian children. They had treated Russian

POWs almost as badly as they had treated the Jews. They had starved and killed millions of them. And now the Russians were coming, getting stronger every day, with nothing but revenge on their minds.

We now know, through the writings and the records of the Nazis themselves, that they were in the process of trying to erase Auschwitz—to eliminate the evidence and the records, to try to bury the truth of the atrocities that had occurred here, and to try to escape responsibility for the greatest place of mass extermination in the history of mankind. In the end, they even tried to blow up the crematoria and gas chambers in Birkenau, to conceal the horrors they had committed there.

We spent about four or five weeks in this new camp. We had no work, no horses to take care of, nothing whatsoever to occupy ourselves. All we could do was hang out and wait, and speculate among ourselves just what the Germans had in store for us. Which made us even more anxious and fearful. When we were working, we could stop thinking for a few minutes at a time, caught up in our tasks, trying to stay a step or two ahead of the guards. Here, we had nothing to do but think. And considering what we had been through up until now, our futures looked none too long—and none too bright.

Even though we couldn't work, we were still given our usual daily food ration. So most of us were at least maintaining our health. It was soon January in Poland, one of the coldest winters they ever had, so we were glad to be able to stay indoors most of the time and at least stay more or less warm. But we knew, from our years of bitter experience, that the Germans always had something planned for us—something that was always worse than what we had endured up until then.

Chapter 28

The March.

One day, toward the end of January—January 23, 1945, to be exact—we were assembled in the Plawy *Appellplatz*. The SS told us we were to be marched to another camp in the West. We gathered our meager possessions, in my case just my clothes and my battered cup, hanging from the dirty string around my neck. A few of the prisoners managed to carry an old blanket draped around their neck, or even a thin mattress, slung over a shoulder, liberated from the barracks we were leaving behind. The SS formed us into a bigger group. The march that the rest of the stable boys and I were pushed into numbered about 1000. At the start, that is.

We began to walk in the biting cold Polish winter, with no food or water. We were marched down a paved road, covered with snow, ice and slush, with farmland on one side and forest on the other. Ahead of us was the endless roadway, disappearing into the distance.

The road was usually elevated a few feet from the level of the forest with big ditches sloping down away from the roadway, designed to keep the road dry in the rain and melting snow. But these ditches soon became mass graves as the thousands of prisoners, in group after group, came marching through.

The rules of the march were simple. If you kept up with the leading group, you might be allowed to live. If you fell back more than ten meters—33 feet—a Nazi guard shot you in the head.

The Nazis used these death marches as an efficient way to move a lot of people quickly and cheaply. And to murder a lot of people without the need to burn or bury their bodies. If 20, 30 or 40% of the prisoners who were marched out of Auschwitz died along the way, so much the better. It simply left fewer people to guard, fewer animals to house, fewer mouths to feed.

All along the way, we could see the bodies of those who had gone before. They were broken, bloodied, slumped and frozen in the ditches as we passed by. Some had their eyes still open, staring up forever into the Polish sky.

The bodies that we passed, the victims of previous marches—men, women and even children—were left to freeze and later rot. If the body fell close to a village, the Nazis reasoned, Polish farmers and villagers might do the job of burying the dead for them. If the bodies were all shot in one place, the Nazis would have to dispose of them. If the dead were simply scattered along the road where they had been murdered, in ones, twos and threes, the Germans could ignore them and move on, leaving the corpses for somebody else to deal with.

I tried not to look. I always tried to keep my eyes forward and down, to keep from attracting a Nazi's attention. But the bodies were everywhere, as if they had been tossed by some careless, giant hand. Like everybody else in this macabre parade I just kept shuffling along, moving as slowly as I could to save energy, but making sure to keep the same pace as the people ahead. And never stop, or slow, or stand out in any way.

When people grew too tired or too sick or too starved to go on they started to drift back behind us. There was nothing I could do to help them. Some would stumble, fall and try to get up, scrambling in a panic to catch up before a bullet came. Some would just walk slower and slower, gradually falling off the back of the formation. And some, overcome by fatigue, the cold, the pain in their feet, and the sheer hopelessness of their ordeal, would simply give up and stop.

The German guards drove behind the march in a *Kübelwagen*, a jeep-like Volkswagen, and waited for their next victim. If a prisoner stopped to help a faltering comrade, even for a few seconds, he would be shot as well. The crime was being caught 10 meters behind the group. The punishment was swift, sure death.

To avoid having to drag the bodies into the ditches themselves, and possibly get their hands dirty with tainted Jewish blood, the Germans would first force their exhausted victims over to the side of the road. Some pleaded for their lives. Some moaned: "No, no, no". Some cried out to God—as if they believed that there was still a God who might hear them. Some screamed. Some just waited, with their eyes closed, for the last hot flash in the brain that would end their misery.

The Germans dispatched each, in turn, with a rifle bullet or a pistol shot to the back of the shaved head. There would be one more crumpled body. A bright splash of red in the snow, quickly turning brown.

I felt like I was caught in a screaming, thrashing nightmare, a nightmare from which I could never awaken. All that day, again and again, I would see another one of our group begin to weaken, Some of the stronger prisoners would sometimes try to help, holding up their weaker comrade long enough to let him regain the energy, or just the will, to live.

Photo: United States Holocaust Memorial Museum

Jewish prisoners on a death march from the Dachau concentration camp near Munich, Germany. The photo was taken secretly by a courageous German civilian in Grünwald, Germany.

But once a person started to run out of gas, there was usually no way to save him. None of us could risk falling behind with a doomed, luckless straggler. It would simply mean that two Jews would die, rather than just one.

Once a prisoner fell out of ranks, it was a matter of minutes before I would hear the crack of a gunshot behind us, echoing through the pine and spruce trees. Every time I heard a shot, I would put my head down a little farther, and try to walk a little faster.

The road passed through small farm villages, far out in the Polish countryside. The villagers would stare at us, numb to the scene they had been witnessing, day after day, as the endless streams of haggard, filthy prisoners from Auschwitz shuffled past. They might as well have been watching cattle being driven to a slaughterhouse.

As I dragged myself along, I stumbled over a small grey can, half-buried in the frozen mud. It was a can of horsemeat, dropped by a careless German soldier. I bent down, snatched it up and hid it in my jacket. I looked around like a thief, to see if a guard or another prisoner had seen it. I couldn't believe my good fortune. It was mine.

I carried the can like a nugget of gold all that day, trying to figure out how in the world I could open it. I had no knife, no can opener. But thinking about it, and feeling it in my hand, concealed in my clothing, kept me going. I might be right on the edge of stumbling, of slowing, of falling to my knees. But I knew if I could somehow open that can, perhaps at night when we would surely stop, I just might make it another few miles. Maybe another day.

I found a small stone and tried to bash the can open when nobody was looking. I tried a strong stick I broke off a passing tree. I tried everything I could think of, but I could not open that stupid, precious steel can. But having something to think about, a tiny goal, with perhaps some nourishment at the end, gave me the push I needed to keep on walking.

We sheltered for the night in a huge barn, my stable-boy friends and I huddled together for warmth. The Nazis gave us no food. No bread. No soup. I clutched my can of meat like a beggar with his last coin, unable to eat it and unable to throw it away.

Chapter 29

Under Attack.

I awoke to another bleak, grey Polish winter day. The Germans barked, prodded and herded us all back into formation, and the insane race started all over again. We had started with about 1000 prisoners, as best as I could estimate. Now there were about 800 or 900 of us still alive. My feet were frozen and torn from trudging through the mud and ice and snow.

In the late afternoon we finally dragged ourselves to a railroad siding. The Germans forced us into open-topped freight cars, packed as tightly as threadbare human bodies can be packed.

There were four cars in the train, with maybe 200 or 250 people crammed into each car. Now we weren't so cold, and being jammed in with everybody else at least gave us a tiny bit of security. It was agonizing, standing for hours without moving, with all those stinking bodies nearly squeezing the breath out of me. But I still had a pulse. I was still alive, unlike so many of the people we had left behind on the road. And still held my precious can of horsemeat under my shirt, giving me a tiny candle of hope.

Each of the open cars had a German guard posted up above, on the rear wall, with a machine gun pointed down at us. There was nothing we could have done to rebel, or escape, but these guys weren't taking any chances.

The train rolled and rocked, clattering on and on. The rumor passed through the car that we were heading toward the west. One of the prisoners said he could tell by the position of the sun, which was hanging low on the left side of the car. This didn't make any sense to us. The Germans had kicked us out of Germany, and tried to kill us so we would not be able to come back. Why in the world, after all this, would they be sending us back toward Germany?

Of course we didn't know about the Red Army overwhelming the German Wehrmacht in the east, and just how badly the war was going for the Germans. We didn't know that just ten days after we left, Auschwitz was overrun by the Russians, and that a few thousand of the weakest, sickest prisoners, the ones who had been judged too weak to be marched to the west, were then liberated. They had been scheduled to be shot by the Auschwitz guards before the Russians arrived, to keep them from revealing the horrors of the gas chambers, the crematoria, and the million or more Jews who had died there.

In the chaos of the German retreat, those last few prisoners had somehow survived. The Nazi guards had been too busy saving their own skins to bother with killing the last few sick, starving Jews. And now those Jews were being fed and clothed and nursed to health by the Russians. No such luck for us. We were just sardines in a can, chugging slowly westward, with no idea of what would become of us.

That night the train stopped at a siding at another concentration camp, *Gross-Rosen*, near the border between Germany and what is now Poland.

In the confusion of the German retreat, we had been sent to *Gross-Rosen* on the assumption that we would be unloaded and imprisoned there. The Commandant of *Gross-Rosen* refused to accept us. The camp was already overcrowded, he protested. So it was decided, we later learned, that we would be kept in the cars and sent even farther to the west the next morning. For me it would be a twisted sort of homecoming. After over three years imprisoned in Poland—in the Lodz Ghetto and in Auschwitz—I was being shipped back to Germany.

I'm not sure how much time passed on the train. I was exhausted and numb, and nearly unconscious from hunger and thirst. I drifted in and out of sleep, nodding with the rocking of the cars and the clatter of the wheels on the tracks.

I woke up to hear a strange roar and throb pouring down from the sky. The German guards above our car got very excited and started firing their machine guns upward, swiveling around to shoot. Hot brass cartridge cases fell down from the guns, tumbling onto the heads of us prisoners underneath.

I strained to see what was happening, but I couldn't make out much with the walls of the train cars towering over my head. There were two very loud, very fast single-engined airplanes wheeling above, apparently lining up to attack. I had no idea of who these airplanes belonged to or where they had come from. I had seen German airplanes with the cross and swastika. But these hurtling, olive-drab-painted planes had big, round red-and-white insignia on their wings and fuselages. I now know that they were British fighter-bombers, probably Hawker Typhoons.

In all the war, ever since we'd left Cologne, this was the first time I had ever seen American or British airplanes. It was the first indication I had that the Allies had invaded Europe and were possibly winning the war, that they had achieved enough dominance over the skies of Germany so that there might be some hope of our being liberated.

But before that, these planes were going to try to kill us. From the air I'm sure our train looked like every other German military troop train. The British pilots had no way of knowing that there were hundreds of innocent prisoners crammed into the open cars. But they could surely see the German gunners up above each car, hammering away with their machine guns, trying to shoot them down.

The planes wheeled over us, then disappeared over the horizon. They came back in attack mode, strafing the train from head on with their roaring 20mm cannons. Hundreds of exploding bullets tore through the cars and the people inside.

I had been one of the first few prisoners who had been jammed into my car. So I was pushed up toward the right front corner, protected a little bit by the front wall of the car.

The prisoners in the rear of our car were not so lucky. A 20mm cannon shell is about the size of your thumb and it's going twice the speed of sound. The shells exploded when they hit, tearing people apart. And because we were packed in so tightly, one shell could kill many prisoners. A boy would be there one second, and then disappear in a burst of blood, bone, cloth and flesh. All this was happening just a few feet away from me.

The German machine gunner, perched up on the back wall of my car, was killed by a walking spray of bullets. He slumped over his gun like a discarded rag doll, his helmet clattering down onto the prisoners, blood pouring from his head.

The fighters kept coming, attacking head-on, trying to explode the engine's boiler, cripple the train, and then finish us off. For all those Allied pilots knew, they were attacking a train full of heavily armed German troops who would be shooting at them, and their British and American comrades, for the rest of the war.

The planes must have run out of fuel or ammunition because one minute they were coming at us, and the next minute the noise had stopped and the train was still chugging along.

The carnage in the back of our car was horrifying. It looked like there had been a bomb in a butcher shop. Dozens of prisoners had been killed, and dozens more were moaning and screaming, dying of their awful wounds, or simply bleeding to death.

The train just kept going, blood streaming out of the cars and onto the tracks. If the train had stopped, or been disabled, we might have all been wiped out by the airplanes.

There was no thought of the Germans providing any help or medical attention. Or even food or water. Or the decency of removing the dead, and the blood, and the body parts from the cars. The grim, battered train just rumbled on through the day and into the night, the living, the dead and the dying still pressed together.

I tried to sleep, curled up on the bloody floor of the rolling, shaking car. Even my can of horsemeat had slipped away, lost in the chaos. I closed my eyes, and tried to hold my arms over my ears—anything to muffle the moans and the horror before they could reach my brain, the place where an innocent Cologne kid named Heinz Oster once lived.

Chapter 30

Buchenwald.

The screeching of the train's wheels on the iron rails shook me awake. I had been curled up in the same position for hours, and had no idea of whether I could ever straighten out again. The German guards outside yanked the rusty doors open, and the survivors of the ride began to tumble out, some landing on their feet, some just falling to the grey gravel train siding. When the open air got to my place in the corner, I half crawled, half rolled across the blood- and urine- and vomit-covered wooden floor toward the door.

I tried to hang my legs over the side of the door to cushion my fall, but my legs simply refused to unfold. A couple fellow inmates took me by the shoulders and set me on the ground, but I still could not stand up.

It was as if there were two huge rubber bands between my butt and my ankles, keeping my legs folded with tremendous pressure. The cramps in my stomach, which had no food in it for days, were so intense that I thought I might be curled that way forever. For hours afterward, I could only hobble around like a cripple, hunched over my knees like a 90-year-old man.

Judging by the number of cars in that train, and how tightly they were packed, it was later estimated that about 800 prisoners had been loaded onto the train after the death march from Auschwitz. Only 400 or so were still alive when we arrived.

"Welcome to Buchenwald." said one of the prisoners unloading the train.

I couldn't believe it. I got kicked out of Germany, thrown into Poland to rot, and now I'm thrown back in the god-forsaken land of my birth. I had a strange connection to Buchenwald. Unlike the other awful places I was sent to, I actually knew something about it. I remembered that my cousin, Walter, had told me all about the place when we were crammed into the tiny apartment in Cologne back in 1939.

As I said before, Walter had left the apartment then and tried to escape from Germany by hiking over the mountains into Switzerland. Before his flight into the mountains, he had come to visit us in Cologne. He told us about how he had been put into Buchenwald after he was captured on November 9, the famous night of broken glass—*Kristallnacht*. He was in the group of 30,000 Jewish men who had been rounded up that night—the roundup my father had escaped because of his relationship with the hotel doorman. The Nazis had set Walter's apartment on fire, so he jumped out the window to try to get away. But they captured him. The next thing he knew, he was a prisoner in Buchenwald.

Walter was forced into slave labor to expand the camp, to build it up and get it ready for all the prisoners who were destined to come. In those days, the Nazis had not yet embarked on the "Final Solution": that is, the systematic extermination of all the Jews of Europe. Back in 1939, if you served a period of time—and if they didn't kill you by beating, or hanging, or shooting, or disease first—they would allow you leave. So my cousin Walter was set free—or as free as a Jew could be in Germany at the time. And he came to visit us in our cramped Cologne apartment at Number 15 Blumenthalstrasse we had been forced into by the Nazis.

He told us about the atrocities he had witnessed in Buchenwald, how unimaginable the conditions were, how ruthless the Germans had been. The release of many of the first concentration camp prisoners was how the German population found out about what was going on, and why they became too frightened to help us. The prisoners who were released from Buchenwald in that first wave of repression told the world. Not that the world paid much attention.

The things Walter told us about the camp, back when I was just an 11-year-old boy in Cologne, were now happening to me. After all I had been through, it made it just a little more horrible, knowing that I was in the exact same place that had frightened me so much when Walter told us about it.

Buchenwald was originally intended to be a camp for political prisoners, rather than a camp like Birkenau, which was designed and built to simply murder people. It was filled, at first, with writers, artists, Communists, and anybody else who might have shown the Nazis the slightest resistance. It was up on a mountain above the city of Weimar, which at one time had been the capital of Germany, in the time of the Weimar Republic. It was built, at first, to be a camp with a reasonable level of civility—it wasn't designed to be as horrible a place as Birkenau or Treblinka. But by 1945, after 6 years of war, and hundreds of thousands of prisoners having lived and, mostly, died there, the conditions had deteriorated tremendously.

We weren't brought there to serve any particular function—they were just storing us there until we died or were killed, to keep us out of the hands of the Russians coming from the East, and the American and British coming from the West. There had been an ammunition factory and a bayonet factory there, both of which were run by slave labor from the camp, but these had been blown up by Allied planes in a series of low-level air attacks before I arrived, in late January of 1945.

Now there was nothing going on here except starving, waiting and dying.

Photo: United States Holocaust Memorial Museum

Appell (roll call) at the Buchenwald concentration camp near Weimar, Germany.

Chapter 31

Whispers In The Night.

After a couple of weeks there, I had made a friend in Buchenwald. He was a teenager named Ivar—Ivar Segalowitz— who slept next to me on our wooden platform. He was from a small German-speaking village in Lithuania, and was a couple years younger than I. We would whisper into the night sometimes, talking about our lives before the war, and what we might do if we ever got out of there. While people all around us were dying, by starvation or disease or by deliberately killing themselves, having a friend was one way we could take our minds off our dreadful existence.

After all these years in the Ghetto and the camps, I had become a pretty hardened little man. I had nobody to help me out but myself, so it was quite a risk to let anybody inside my brittle shell. It was hard to have any meaningful human contact in the camps. Like a soldier who doesn't want to risk becoming friends with a new replacement, it was best not to have too much feeling for another prisoner, because he was probably going to be dead in a few days or weeks anyway. Why risk the emotional effort? Why risk your own will to keep going?

Back in Auschwitz it had been pretty much every man and boy for himself. But here, for some reason, Ivar and I allowed ourselves the luxury of becoming close friends. If nothing else, I thought, if even one of us survived to remember the other, it would be better than both of us just disappearing off the face of the earth, as so many had before us.

Ivar's education and upbringing were not as strong as mine had been. I was originally from a well-to-do German family, raised in a big, very cosmopolitan German city. So even after all these years of starvation and persecution, I still had a few shreds of self-esteem. I had a little bit of my identity left, I guess you could say, even after 11 years of the Nazis telling me I was subhuman vermin.

Ivar was not so lucky. He was from a farming village in a less-sophisticated, more-rural country, and had not had the same kind of schooling and cultural background as I had. So his idea of himself, his self-perception, was perhaps not as strong as mine in those days of hopelessness and starvation. If everyone around you seems to hate you, year after year, it's not hard to start to think that they might be right after all.

Ivar was sure he was going to die. He had been through so much hell, and had seen so many lose their minds and give up. He was feeling emotionally weaker and weaker as the strength drained out of his body—he had barely survived a bout with typhoid fever, which was rolling through the camp, killing hundreds. He was teetering on the edge of giving up.

I did the best I could to prop him up, to encourage him to keep on going for another hour, another day, maybe another week. My seeing Ivar as a kind of little brother, adopting him in a small way, helped me just as much as it helped him, I believe. And because we were among the very few kids in the camp who spoke German as a first language, we had an immediate bond. We were called *Yekkes*—German Jews— by the other kids—and not in a kind, understanding way. So together we formed our own little gang, our tiny fraternity of two.

If I was busy trying to keep his spirits up, to convince him that we both might come out of this mess in the end, I had less time to think about myself. You can't very well give up hope while you're trying to convince somebody else not to give up hope. So we slogged on, a little pair of starving Jewish boys, our own tiny conspiracy against the world of Buchenwald.

With their bizarre sense of cruelty the Germans couldn't stand to see anyone not being worked to death. So they would occasionally send Ivar and me, along with the rest of our barracks, to a nearby quarry.

There was no useful work to be done. The Germans just ordered us to carry rocks from the bottom of the quarry to the top. And when we were done, they forced us to carry the rocks back down to the bottom. They did this just to punish us—for being Jewish, I suppose. Just to make sure we were still doing hard labor. Because if we died from exhaustion, or starvation, or an accident in the quarry, they wouldn't have to waste a bullet, or give some poor German soldier nightmares if he was forced to shoot us.

It became known after the war that one of the major reasons the

Germans built the gas chambers at Birkenau, Treblinka, and many of the other extermination camps was that shooting innocent men, women and children took a huge emotional toll on some of the German soldiers themselves.

After a few months on an *Einsatzgruppen* detail—the bands of *Waffen SS* soldiers who roamed over Eastern Europe in the early stages of the war, shooting Russian prisoners, Gypsies and Jews into mass graves the doomed civilians had just dug for themselves—many of the soldiers were psychologically destroyed. It turns out that killing people day in and day out can be nearly as destructive to a human's emotional and mental health as being shot at himself.

Every now and then some of the other prisoners would be sent down in teams to the city of Weimar, to help clean up the damage from the nighttime bombing raids, which were happening a little more frequently as time passed by. They would help to clean up the rubble, piling the bricks next to the road so the buildings could start to be rebuilt. They would also pick up and bury the corpses of the casualties: old men, women, children—civilians, mostly—who had been killed in the previous night's air raid. It was horrifying, dirty, exhausting work, of course. You don't have to bury many children before you feel the experience starting to gnaw away at your soul. But at least it gave those guys the opportunity to scrounge for some extra food. I never got to go on one of those assignments. I never knew why. Perhaps because the guards knew I spoke German, which might make it easier for me to escape and to lose myself in the city.

The guys who did go tried to find food where ever they could in the shattered buildings, but there simply wasn't much around to be had. The German civilians weren't as bad off as we were, but they were starting to starve too by then.

There was a German writer imprisoned there in Buchenwald, a fellow inmate who had been there for four years, since 1941. He was called Georg, but I don't remember his last name. I met him in the bathroom, which was one of the few places you could talk freely with an inmate from another barrack without causing suspicion.

He had been treated much better than we Jews had, which is why he had survived all these years. He was being held there strictly because of his political views, and political prisoners were viewed as being more worthy of humane treatment than us Jews. He was an older man, then in his late 40s. He had a clandestine radio, and some other privileges and connections with the underground camp leaders that let him roam around the camp as he pleased. He also had a friend in the administration, which allowed him to find out what was going on outside the gates. He was one of the few inmates there who actually had some idea of what was coming.

I was pretty much at the end of my rope by then. I had been starved and shot at and worked nearly to death for all these years. I had been lucky so far, to have made it all this time. But just like Ivar's, my body—and, to be honest, my will to live—had just about been used up.

I guess my condition was obvious to Georg. He had seen so many prisoners come in on the trains, and go out up the chimney of the crematorium. "Hold on," Georg told me, there in the stinking latrine. "Whatever you do, hold on."

"I don't know what it means to 'hold on,'" I said.

"Don't give up," he said. He couldn't tell me anything specific, because that would have been a huge risk for him. But hearing that one bit of encouragement, after being worn down and starved for so long, might have been one of the reasons I'm still here to tell the story.

He must have known, through his connections in the camp, what was happening just to the west. He must have known that General George Patton's Third Army was rushing toward us, and that the German Wermacht and Luftwaffe were getting weaker every day. The Germans were running out of fuel and tanks and ammunition and men. Patton and his tanks were rushing full speed into the heart of Germany, and there was not much the German supermen could do to stop them.

Chapter 32

The Negroes Are Coming!

We did see two small, slow airplanes one day, circling slowly below us, working their way down the forested hill toward the city. We could see pieces of paper trailing out and fluttering down. They were leaflets, dropped by the small US Army Air Corps planes as a part of their psychological warfare efforts, to try to convince the Germans to give up and surrender. I didn't know any of this at the time. I had no idea that the Allies had invaded Europe and were heading our way. We simply had no information, no word from the outside world at all.

I later found out that the leaflets we saw being dropped on Weimar were some of General Patton's most ingenious propaganda weapons. American psychologists had decided that the way to demoralize a German soldier was to attack his manhood.

But if they proclaimed that German soldiers were unmanly—cowards or homosexuals—they realized that this tactic would make the Germans even angrier, and fight even harder, to prove that they were real men. They reasoned that this might make them less likely to surrender—exactly the opposite effect they were trying to achieve.

The psychologists decided to threaten what the Germans saw as their strength—their masculinity itself. These guys had been told that they were rough, tough supermen since they were 10 or 12 years old. There's nothing more important to a superman, said the psychologists, than protecting his testicles.

The leaflets told these elite Wehrmacht and SS men that they were going to be fighting, hand to hand, against black African-American troops. The leaflets were created to appeal to the Germans' racism and fear of the unknown. They showed a black American soldier, drawn by some U.S. Army cartoonist, as a drooling monster with huge bulging eyes, big heavy lips, sharp wolf-like teeth and a snarling, menacing face. It was pretty racist, now that I think about it. But I don't think many of our black soldiers would have objected to being portrayed as a Nazi's worst nightmare.

In one hand, this leering black GI held a huge knife, dripping with blood. And in the other hand, a severed white penis and a pale pair of testicles.

The Germans had been taught all these years that black Africans were subhuman, blood-thirsty barbarians. That they were cannibals. And now that the Nazis had their backs against the wall, watching their comrades and families bombed and shot and starved, they believed they were up against drooling black ape-men who might be more interested in cutting off their balls than taking them prisoner.

This became a powerful motivation for the Germans to give themselves up. Especially if they could find a nice, familiar, white American soldier to surrender to.

There actually were a fair number of black American troops in segregated units fighting in Patton's army, which was bearing down from the west toward Weimar and Buchenwald. There was an entirely black tank battalion, the 761st, which was one of the best-trained and most-effective armored battalions in the U.S. Army. There were also units of

Photo: US Department of Defense

African-American tankers of the 761st Tank Battalion, US 3rd Army

black combat engineers in the area, helping to establish bases and keep Pattons' armored and infantry divisions supplied as they raced across Germany toward Berlin.

Black American troops destroyed many German tanks, and killed many German soldiers. But the historical record shows that, despite Patton's brutally effective propaganda, the great majority of those unfortunate German soldiers went to their reward with their testicles still attached.

Chapter 33

Lying With the Dead.

I had been there in Buchenwald a little over two months, through February and March, when the food and water stopped altogether. It was as if these Germans who had been so concerned with imprisoning and exterminating us all had now just forgotten that we were there.

There was a sense of foreboding. A sense of doom. Ivar and I were trapped in this stinking place without any form of sustenance whatsoever. If we stayed, we would die. If we tried to escape, we would be shot.

When the food stopped coming, people started dying all over the place. They just stopped living, wherever they happened to be. Where before, our section of Buchenwald had been a more-or-less-organized hell, it was now turning into an unending scene of filth, death and despair.

When somebody died the Germans didn't even take them away. The bodies just laid there in their bunks, sometimes for days. We inmates didn't have the strength to move them, and the Germans wouldn't allow it anyway. So the barracks turned into these bizarre mausoleums, filled with the living lying next to the dead.

The damned Germans' solution was to throw chlorine powder onto the dead bodies to keep them from completely decomposing. The choking chlorine fumes forced those of us who were still alive to crowd into the upper bunks, away from the stink and the disease. I can still feel the searing of the chlorine in my lungs—it was there all the time, day in and day out. To this day, if I go to a swimming pool and get a whiff of that chlorine smell, it takes me right back to that awful barracks: Block 66.

At night, we were completely closed in. If we went outside to take a breath or two the Germans would shoot. Which, when things looked so endless and so hopeless, didn't seem so bad. A few steps outside into the clear night air, and then a bang or two that would end my pain.

I managed to find a tiny dormer window, up in the top tier of the bunks, where I could catch a few breaths. There was a small iron rod I could push to prop the window open, and Ivar and our other bunkmates took turns at night, breathing through this tiny opening to keep from suffocating. It was like we were taking the last few breaths of air before we went down with our sinking ship.

This went on for ten days. No food. Almost no water. No nothing. After a few days, I lost the little strength I had. My stomach had shrunk so much again, into a knot, that I couldn't even straighten up. I was a 16-year-old boy who looked like an emaciated 100-year-old man, curled in a ball on a rough wooden bunk. There was no sanitation at all. The rotting bodies, and all the filth from those of us who were still alive, made the barracks impossible to live in. The bodies drew flies and maggots and lice. But there was nothing we could do but wait.

I did see Georg once during those last few days. "Now more than ever," he told me. "Have the courage to keep on going."

"Don't give up," he said to me. "It will soon be over."

"Well", I thought. "Over for him? Maybe over for me? What do I know?"

Chapter 34

A Tank with the Star of David.

A day or two after I last spoke to Georg, I was lying on my bunk next to Ivar, trying not to starve to death. I was so weak I couldn't move, and there was no reason to move anyway. We hadn't seen food for ten days.

We had been told, through the camp grapevine—messages whispered in passing on the *Appelplatz*, or in the latrine—that the Germans had been rounding up Jewish prisoners and sending them away on trains or on death marches, or taking them out into the woods to be shot, in a last-minute effort to silence the witnesses. We were weak, helpless and terrified. We didn't have the strength to move, let alone run or fight. So all we could do was hide in our barracks, try not to be noticed, and keep on breathing.

It was about three o 'clock on the afternoon of April 11. We heard something outside the barrack that we had not heard before: a roaring, rattling sound which seemed to be getting closer.

One of the guys in my barrack, one of the few who could still stand up for a few minutes at a time, got up to look out one of the shoulder-high windows. Then he said, in a small, broken voice: "I think we're being liberated."

We didn't believe him. I had seen so many people go over the edge, over all the years of my imprisonment, that it was hard for me to take him seriously. You never knew what to believe, and what not to believe. Prisoners lost it and went insane all the time. I'd seen people throw themselves against electric wire, just to end their own suffering. This was probably just one more inmate cracking up. Tomorrow, it might be me. I'd seen it hundreds of times. Why should I get my hopes up? Why should I move a muscle? Why would this be any different?

He kept on rasping. "If you don't believe me, come and take a look."

"What the hell," I thought. Along with some of the other guys, I moved slowly to the dirty, broken panes.

I could see a tank coming, a big olive-colored monster roaring up the road between the barracks. We had heard that the Germans had orders to obliterate the camp if there was any chance of its being captured. We believed that they would never let us out into the world, never let us tell our stories. So when I first saw the tanks coming I was sure that this was it, that the Germans were here to blow us all up.

Where I expected to see a white and black German cross, as on every tank I'd ever seen, there was the Jewish star of David, scrawled in chalk on the side of this tall, frightful machine.

"Why would the Germans pull a prank like this?" I asked myself. We had no idea, even in April of 1945, that Europe had been invaded by the Allies, that the American Third Army was roaring through western Germany, or that Germany was on the edge of defeat. Except for those few words from my friend Georg, which really told me nothing, I had no clue about what had been going on in the outside world.

I did know that I was weak and dizzy. If it wasn't for the window sill I was leaning against, I would fall down in a heap.

"I'm hallucinating too," I thought.

The officer on top of the tank turret was wearing a greenish-brown uniform, which did not look familiar to me—German Wehrmacht or SS uniforms were almost always grey or black. I realized that he was yelling in Yiddish, which no German officer would ever do.

"*Ihr seit fray!*" he cried, again and again. "You are free!"

"*Meir zeinen aher kehn makhn`du fray!*" he yelled, as inmates started to stir from their starvation-induced stupor.

"We have come here to make you free!"

A murmur and shuffle started behind me. Ivar dragged himself off our wooden pallet like a corpse coming to life and crawling out of its casket. Any prisoner who could still move started walking, crawling or dragging himself along the dirt floor, scuffling toward the windows, falling out the door.

The word spread from bunk to bunk, from barrack to barrack. People had been dying so fast that there was no way to know who was still with us, and who was gone. The living tried to wake the dead next to them, anxious to tell them the news.

The world was a staggering jumble of faded blue and dirty-white stripes. Those of us who could walk shuffled out into the daylight, dumbfounded that there were no Germans around to shoot us or beat us or work us to death. The stronger ones helped the weaker ones up and out of their sleeping racks and out into the light. Like death-row inmates who had been waiting to die for years, the idea that we really, truly might be free was almost impossible to understand.

We had been liberated by the Third Army, under General George Patton. They had approached the camp with tanks and a few infantrymen, because they thought they might encounter resistance from the Germans. But when it became clear that all of the Nazis had fled, they tore through the barbed wire fences and sent a few tanks up the hill to bring us the message that we had been freed.

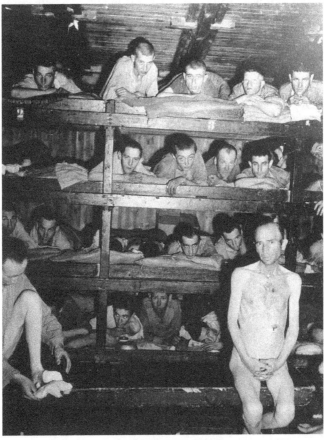

Photo: United States Holocaust Memorial Museum

Liberated Jewish prisoners, Buchenwald concentration camp, April 1945.

Chapter 35

The well, the sick and the dying.

I was lying on the ground in front of our barrack, trying to understand that it was really over. I was curled up in a ball, paralyzed by weakness and the stomach cramps that come with near-starvation. But I was alive. The scene was total chaos. Some prisoners were delirious. There was screaming, crying, shouting everywhere.

More and more Americans started to appear, driving up the hill in their jeeps and trucks. They hadn't come prepared to rescue tens of thousands of starving skeletons, so they tried to give us any food they could spare. I remember one GI gave me a stick of chewing gum. I had no idea what chewing gum was, so I tried and tried to eat it, but it just wouldn't dissolve. I didn't know what to do with it, so I finally just swallowed it whole.

Another soldier gave me a tin of some kind of meat—I guess it must have been Spam. It was the best thing I had ever tasted. The Americans started to get more organized as the afternoon turned into evening. Medics came and started the process of triage: separating the prisoners into three groups.

The first group were the healthiest: men who didn't need immediate medical attention. The second group was composed of men and boys who desperately needed help—food, and water, and medical attention—but who would probably survive.

The third group was the dying. Even though they were alive, and they were free, that didn't mean that they would live to see the next day. It was the medics' terrible job to decide who they could save, and who they could not. There were very meager supplies that first night, and a limited number of people to care for the worst cases. Many boys and men died that first night before the food and clean water and medicine could save them.

Somehow my friend Ivar, who was barely able to stand, was selected to be treated. He was, at the time, what the Germans in the camps would call a *musselman*—their crude, intolerant way of saying that he was too far gone to save. But the Americans disagreed and selected him to be treated, probably because of his size and his youth.

Once we were divided by our medical condition, the American medics and soldiers separated us boys out from the rest of the population. I guess they had decided that we were a priority to keep alive, for the same reason the Germans had tried to kill as many young Jews as possible. Because we represented the next generation of an entire people.

An officer walked us, slowly and painfully, out of the barbed-wire prisoner complex and over to the stone buildings, with real heat and light, where the German SS guards had been living. It was dirty and run down, but it looked like a palace to us. Most of the kids—myself included—got their own personal bunk bed to sleep on.

The German SS officers had slept in double bunks, while the enlisted men slept three-high. I was lucky enough to wind up in an officers' barrack, in one of the double bunks. This was the first mattress I had slept on since we had been forced out of our apartment in Cologne back in1935. Ten years of sleeping on bare wood.

Of course we were all as hungry as hell. And as we gathered our strength, we started to gain the courage to complain to our hosts, these overfed Americans who were running around trying to keep order.

Because we were children and teenagers, the Americans still exerted complete control over us. They refused to give us much to eat that first night for fear that a sudden, unrationed intake of food would overwhelm our starved digestive systems, and do more harm than good. This seemed ridiculous to us. We were starving and we needed food. Every cell in my body was screaming out for bread, for meat, potatoes, cheese—anything I could get my hands on. But the medics calmly, insistently said no. They said we would be given small amounts, a little more each day, in order to make sure we didn't die from the trauma of too much, too soon.

I'm grateful that they did. The grown men who were liberated that day were completely free, though the Americans tried to keep all the prisoners corralled in the camp to make sure there wasn't any interference with the war effort, and to make sure some overeager American machine gunner or fighter pilot didn't mistake them for German troops and shoot them.

But a lot of the healthier prisoners had already flown the coop. Some of these prisoners were Russian POWs: prisoners of war. They had been housed in a separate subcamp, divided from ours by barbed wire. These guys were, for the most part, in better shape than we were. The Nazis had, at least during my time in Buchenwald, treated them with some semblance of legality, giving at least lip service to the idea of treating military prisoners within the laws of the Geneva Convention. But like us they had still been starving for the last ten days or so.

Many of these Russians, German Communists and political prisoners went kind of crazy. Because they were adults and our allies the U.S. military had no official power over where they went, or what they did.

A lot of them had already fled the camp by the time the Americans arrived, or soon thereafter. They were running all over the area, gathering food where ever they could, mostly in the form of livestock they had "liberated" from the local farms.

They brought sheep and cows and pigs and chickens back to the camp, slaughtered them, and then cooked up an immense meal in the huge camp kitchen. They ate like pigs, which was exactly what every one of us wanted to do.

The result was horrifying. Hundreds of these guys were overcome by the assault on their systems of all that greasy food. Their stomachs, like

Photo: United States Holocaust Memorial Museum

Buchenwald survivor, April 11, 1945

mine, had shrunken down to where they could hardly process anything at all. If you don't eat for a long time an onslaught of food can simply block up and overwhelm the system, sending you into shock and, for many people, death. Which is what happened to many of those poor, ravenous Russians and other older prisoners. They keeled over and died horrible, painful deaths, the victims of their own animal hunger. Their bodies lay there in the *Appellplatz*—some living, many of them not—on the very day they had been freed.

Back in our own converted SS barrack the evening quickly gave way to night. The healthier kids were chattering back and forth as the lights came on, starting to act a little like teenaged boys again. As the adrenaline of our liberation started to wear off, I was overcome with fatigue and weakness and slipped off to sleep—the first time in what seemed like a lifetime I could go to sleep knowing that I was going to be free in the morning.

Chapter 36

Behind the Wire at Buchenwald.

In our research for this book we learned that in the last few days before the Americans arrived the Russians and other Communist prisoners had essentially taken over control of their section of Buchenwald. They had hidden secret caches of weapons in various places all over the camp.

There had been a tense standoff between the Communists, who ran the camp inside the barbed wire, and the SS and SS *Oberführer* Hermann Pister, the camp Commandant, who was a weak man, prone to delaying decisions, and who realized that the American military advance across Germany made the liberation of Buchenwald just a matter of time.

The Communists had known that Heinrich Himmler, the Nazi chief of the SS, had ordered all prisoners to be killed and the camps destroyed. But the Communist inmates had very good intelligence on what was happening on the outside, and they did everything they could to slow down the SS, and keep as many Jews and other camp inmates safe as long as they could—especially us children.

Even so, many Jews were killed in those last few days. On April 7, just 4 days before the liberation, a train had been loaded with Jews marched out of Buchenwald and sent to the east, toward the Dachau concentration camp near Munich. The train finally arrived there on April 27th. In that time a huge number of the Jews on board had starved, died from illness, or had been strafed by Allied fighter planes, just as my train had been a few months before.

In their standoff with the Germans the camp inmate leaders knew that even with their cache of weapons they were no match for the 3000 or so SS guards if an all-out rebellion broke out. But by refusing to assemble when told by the Nazis, they hoped to slow down the Nazi killing machine until the Allies could make it to the camp and liberate us. They had even improvised a radio transmitter and were sending out a frantic series of SOS messages, encouraging the Americans to come as soon as possible.

At one point the Nazis, tipped off by a turncoat within the camp, tried to assemble 46 of the most active prisoner leaders to be taken away and shot. But with their excellent spy network within the camp, the inmate underground managed to hide almost all those on the list, underneath barracks or in other secret places, or exchange their identities with prisoners who had already died, making it nearly impossible for the SS to tell who was who, and whom to shoot.

Another time in those last days, the word came down that the few English and American prisoners in the camp were to be executed. They were hidden in burrows and dugout hiding places underneath barracks all over the camp, and supplied with food and water by the other inmates whenever the Nazis turned their backs.

As young Jews who had just recently arrived in Buchenwald my fellow teenagers and I were not a part of any of this. We were closed off in the Little Camp, the worst part of the complex, and had no idea that

Photo: U.S. Department of Defense

Victims of the Dachau Death Train, which left Buchenwald for the Dachau concentration camp, near Munich, Germany, on April 7, 1945, just four days before Buchenwald was liberated by the US 3rd Army. Henry Oster was subjected to the same conditions in a similar car on the trip from Auschwitz to Buchenwald.

all this was happening. The inmate leaders didn't know if they could trust any of us. When people are as desperate to live as we were, they will do just about anything, including informing on their fellow prisoners, for a crust of bread. We were new and weak and by that time we were in such sorry shape that we wouldn't have been much good in a fight anyway.

But as the tensions in the camp had grown, we were hearing through the camp grapevine that every now and then the Nazis ordered groups of Jews and others to report to the *Appellplatz*, probably to be taken away to death marches or to be shot in the woods.

In my particular corner of the camp we did everything we could to keep our heads down. To appear not to exist—a skill I had been perfecting for years in Auschwitz.

Chapter 37

The SS on the Run.

A few days before April 11th the Germans seemed to get the idea that staying around Buchenwald was not going to be good for their health. They abandoned their posts and tried to slip away, some of them discarding their SS uniforms and putting on civilian clothes to try to evade the Allied soldiers and the revenge-crazy inmates of the camp.

On that day of liberation, some of the Russian POWs went chasing the escaping SS guards up into the forests and fields to the north, and south down the hill toward the city of Weimar. Quite a few of the SS guys didn't survive. The Russians were intent on getting their revenge. The Germans had been especially brutal on the Eastern Front, and these Russians were in no mood to let the Germans off easily.

Many of the SS guards were caught and beaten and kicked to death by the Russians, or by German Communists who had also been imprisoned. We found out later that some of the guards were lynched by revenge-seeking prisoners. They had been hanged from trees, right where they were captured.

In fact, the first Americans to enter Buchenwald found the camp by accident. It was the crew of a 3rd Army armored car, commanded by a Captain Frederic Keffer, which was assigned to scout the area in the fields and forest north of Weimar.

They spotted a group of SS guards who were running from the camp, followed by a bunch of escaped Russian prisoners who were trying to catch them and kill them. The Russians told the American scouting squad where the camp was, and a couple of the Russians hopped onto the armored car—which looked like a small tank with wheels—to act as guides on the way through the barbed wire and into the camp.

So the first Americans to enter the camp were Captain Keffer and his assistant, Technical Sergeant Herbert Gottshalk, a Jewish-American

GI. They left their armored car with two other G.I.s outside the camp and walked into the compound through a hole in the barbed wire on the north side of the compound. They were greeted by a scene of total chaos, of thousands of prisoners celebrating their salvation.

Some of the stronger prisoners, according to Captain Keffer's account, lifted the Americans into the air by their arms and legs and threw them into the air in joy, again and again. Captain Keffer was tossed about so violently that he grew dizzy, and had to ask the prisoners to stop their crazy demonstration of their freedom.

I didn't witness this myself: my barrack was not near where these first two entered the camp, so we didn't get the word until a little bit later, when a small squadron of U.S. tanks ran over the barbed wire on the south and roared into the middle of the camp.

Chapter 38

Black and White.

When I woke up, the morning after our liberation, it took me a few
minutes to realize that this was not just another dream, one that I would
soon awake from, and find myself plunged back into the nightmare my
life had been for so many years.

It was really true that I was on a warm, soft mattress, all by myself.
I was nudged awake by the commotion around me, of teenagers waking
up and crawling out of the beds. One thing was missing. There were no
shouting Germans. There was nobody ordering me to do anything—a
very strange experience. It was as if I had gone deaf in the night.

I was still very weak, and incredibly hungry. But like all the other boys,
I soon staggered outside into the *Appellplatz* for the morning roll call.

This was very different from every roll call we had undergone before.
Because for once, after all those dark, bleak mornings, and the years of
constant fear of being beaten or worse, every second of every day, we were
lining up this time of our own free will.

The American medics and other soldiers were struggling to get things
organized, and to decide how to take care of all of Buchenwald's 21,000
liberated prisoners. So there was a lot going on, unfolding before our
bewildered, skeletal faces.

It was very hard, at first, to learn to trust these new soldiers, after
having been brutalized for years by German SS, German criminals, and
other Eastern European guards. The Americans seemed very strange to
us, as if they had parachuted down from another planet. And I'm sure
we looked just as bizarre to them. Most of us didn't really look human,
after all we had been through. We were filthy, starved, clothed in rags
or nothing, and spoke a mishmash of different languages, none of them
English.

Different groups of U.S. Army soldiers, medics and others were arriving all the time in jeeps and huge, roaring olive-drab trucks with big white five-pointed stars on the doors.

The first American soldiers we saw on the first day, the ones in the Sherman tanks and the first medics, were white. But the first foot soldiers we encountered the next morning were black Americans. I had never seen a black person before, so that added to the shock and the strangeness of what was happening to us.

Convoys of troops came up to see the horrors of the camp and to help us in any way they could. Some trucks carried white soldiers and some carried black soldiers. But we would never see black and white troops together.

The white Americans were doing the best they could to improve our conditions, but I got the sense that some of them didn't want to get too close, to get too involved with us. I guess I can understand—we were stinking, strange, desperate people, with who knows what diseases. Typhoid fever had been prowling the camp for weeks, and my friend Ivar had barely survived it. And I know now that the American troops had been trained to avoid fraternizing with the local people they encountered throughout the war, to avoid getting sick, to prevent accidental slips of information that might be useful to the enemy, and to avoid becoming emotionally involved, and thus less able to do their jobs as soldiers.

But the black soldiers were wonderful to us. It was clear from the start that they were inherently more generous in how they treated us. They gave every bit of food they could possibly scrounge up and then went looking for more.

Some of them were crying at the horrors they were seeing. And if you've never before seen a black person, it's even more astounding to see a huge, muscular black man, standing in the middle of this barbed-wire prison, with tears streaming down his face. I'm sure it was because the African-American soldiers could hardly overlook the irony of their segregated, second-class status in their own army. Like us, they had been considered inferior beings, sub-human, even as they were fighting the Nazi forces whose philosophy was based on a tragic idea of their racial supremacy.

Even though we could have scarcely been more different, we Jews and these black soldiers had something very special in common. From the opposite sides of the planet, from the first time they drove up that hill it was as if we were somehow, against all logic, part of the same persecuted, misunderstood team—that there was an instant kinship between us.

That feeling of empathy has remained strong within me ever since.

Chapter 39

The First Breakfast.

After the roll call we were ushered into a makeshift dining hall to have our first real meal. The medics were being careful about what, and how much, they were feeding us, which was especially important after the tragedy of the night before, when all those older prisoners had essentially eaten themselves to death.

We each got a cup of milk, a small slice of bread and a single hard-boiled egg. We yelled, we screamed, we cried and complained. And it was kind of liberating in its own right, having the ability to complain to somebody without fear of winding up at the end of a rope, or in a ditch with a hole in your head. But no matter how much noise we made, that was all we got, at least from the camp kitchen that first morning.

In those first couple of days the Americans went to work to assess our health status, to help decide who needed what medical procedures or special treatment. As a part of that we all had to stand in a line to see a medic, who did the best he could to determine the state of our health and record it.

Because of being starved for so many years, I had never really gone through puberty. My body had never had the extra strength to go through the sexual changes that most normal kids go through when they are much younger.

I was 16 years old, but I had the body of a 13-year-old boy. A very skinny 13-year-old boy.

I was weighed then, as part of that first exam. I weighed 78 pounds. About the same weight as a healthy German Shepherd.

Photo: United States Holocaust Memorial Museum

Teenaged survivors, Buchenwald
concentration camp, April, 1945

Chapter 40

Fear of Freedom.

As I slowly regained my strength over the next few days and started to get used to the fact that I might actually have a future, I realized that I was not nearly as happy as I had imagined I would have been. I was terrified.

After years in prison, some convicts find that they really don't know what to do when they are suddenly free. Their lives had been terrible in prison. But at least there, in that controlled environment, they knew what the rules were. Their needs were taken care of by an outside force—even if that force was brutal in the extreme. That happens to people who were fully grown adults when they went into prison, and who were sent to prison for something they had actually done wrong.

I had grown up in the Ghetto of Lodz, and in Auschwitz, and in Buchenwald. Learning how to survive, one awful day after another in the concentration camps, was the only life I had ever known. As hideous as it sounds, Lodz, Auschwitz and Buchenwald had been my only home, and were now my only family.

Now I was free. And very much alone. There were thousands of people around me, of course. But when I looked into the future, staring out from the camp that day at the green, endless world down the hill, I had no idea of what I was going to do, or where I was going to go. I had no idea of who I was.

I was an undeveloped sixteen-year-old boy who the world seemed all-too-eager to abuse and extinguish. All the people and institutions I had ever trusted in my life had been powerless to help me.

Germans had tried to kill me in a number of different ways. They had murdered my mother and father and probably my entire family. Even Allied pilots had shot at me, and ripped apart people standing next to me in that blood-soaked boxcar on the way to Buchenwald.

These new American soldiers and medics and, now, a few American
Army rabbis and social workers from Jewish organizations, seemed better
than the Germans they had replaced. But I had been told a thousand
times before that the people running things were on my side, that
everything was going to turn out fine. It had just never been true.

Now even the hell I had known, that had been my only world for all
this time, had been taken from me too. I couldn't even depend on being
starved, brutalized and persecuted.

I wasn't the only one who didn't know what the future held in store.
The Americans and their allies were busy fighting a war, and having to
suddenly take care of tens of thousands of helpless people at the same
time was not something they had planned for. It seemed that they were
doing as good a job as they could under the circumstances. But I was
constantly afraid that their good nature and intentions would wear off,
that they would become tired of caring for me and the rest of us, and that
things could go back to the way they had been.

Every person and institution in my life had disappeared, abandoned
me, or simply tried to wipe me and my fellows off the face of the earth. I
had learned to never, ever trust anyone or anything. That was one of the
reasons I was still alive. And now, because the uniforms have changed, I
was suddenly supposed to open myself up and give my trust to this army,
this country, these people who spoke this strange new language?

We were in the middle of Germany, but the German people weren't
about to take care of me. They were my tormentors, my mortal enemies.
And they were being bombed and shelled and starved themselves by then.

I had no education, no family, no money, no real clothes. I didn't
even have a country to go home to. I was already there, and it had done
everything in its power to extinguish me and everybody I had ever
known.

I guess now you would call what I was feeling post-traumatic stress
syndrome. At the time, it just felt like soul-numbing, all-pervading dread.

Chapter 41

The Long Road.

The Americans tried their best to help us, first by feeding us increasing portions of the best food they could find, giving us medical attention and rest, and then allowing us to get enough exercise to calm down our newly growing, suddenly hormone-filled bodies.

We were a crazy, uncivilized, unpredictable bunch of boys and young men. Some psychologists who studied us later had the opinion that we might well be unsaveable. That we might have been so emotionally broken and damaged that we would all turn into psychopaths, with no connection to society, and no feeling for anybody but ourselves.

In those first days there was a tornado of activity around Buchenwald. There were soldiers everywhere. Trucks and trucks of food and supplies drove up the hill from Weimar and unloaded at the kitchen. We had never seen so much food: stacks and stacks of flour and sugar and cans of cooking oil. Huge tin containers of milk, in row after row.

There was a Jewish-American chaplain in the camp, Rabbi Herschel Schacter, who had arrived on that first day of liberation just a matter of hours behind the first GIs. He did everything he could to organize the relief efforts and to establish a sense of normalcy and sanity for all the Jews in the camp. He was a kind of intermediary between the Jews and the American military authorities because he could speak Yiddish.

Even though I had been brought up in the Jewish faith in my youth, my subsequent experiences with the Germans had not done anything to instill any belief in a higher power. Through Rabbi Shacter, the Americans were doing everything they could to help us few remaining Jewish children cope with our ordeal, and recover some small sense of normalcy and culture. The Rabbi went through the camp passing out matzo, unleavened bread, because Passover had occurred just a week or so before the camp was liberated.

Once we were allowed to eat without restraint, we took full advantage of the opportunity. We would inhale in a few minutes a meal that would take an hour for a normal person. And I remember never quite believing that there would still be food tomorrow, even though there was plenty of food here today. I had trained myself so well to hoard every crumb of food that I couldn't help myself. I would stuff bread and rolls and chunks of meat into my clothes at mealtimes, to make sure I had some later at night. I would stash food in my clothes, under the blankets of my bed. We all did it.

I felt guilty doing this. I had been conditioned to feel ashamed about anything that was good for me, that would help me survive, for all these years. If I was taking it for myself, I was stealing it from the Reich—and I was always looking over my shoulder when I did.

So even now, when the generous American GIs were more than happy to give us anything they could, we were still behaving like we expected all this good fortune to melt away, to disappear any moment, like a wonderful love dream that you know, somewhere in the back of your mind, that you will soon have to wake up from.

The Americans thought that the best way to treat the worst cases of starvation and dysentery was to give transfusions of blood to the worst-off prisoners, which they did on a massive scale. Many of the Americans who came to the camp wound up in a hospital bed themselves for a few minutes, donating blood so that more of us helpless prisoners could live.

There had been a typhus epidemic in the camp that was still going on when our liberation occurred. The Americans were very brave to expose themselves to this disease, and quite a few were infected.

The Americans had good supplies of the new sulfa drugs that could cure the disease, so it wasn't as bad an affliction for many of them as it had been for us. And the drugs were what saved Ivar, without a shadow of a doubt. The disease has a tendency to affect memory, so for the rest of his life Ivar had a hard time remembering those days, even though he was still sharp and vital 70 years later.

The second day of our liberation was a dark day for the Americans who were working so hard to help us, and try, in their own way, to make up for the ordeal we had been through. Though we really didn't understand much about it, we learned that on that day, April 12, 1945, their leader and commander had died: Franklin Delano Roosevelt, the president who had led America into and through World War ll.

Without Franklin Roosevelt and the American war effort he had created and led for all the years I had been imprisoned, I would never have lived to tell the story.

Chapter 42

The Good Germans Of Weimar.

After seeing the horrors of the nearby Ordruff camp, which had been liberated a few days before, and then witnessing Buchenwald itself, General Eisenhower had decided to force the German civilians of the nearby towns and cities—any civilians within 25 miles—to come up and see what their beloved Führer and their sons and husbands and brothers had created.

The Germans, mostly older, supposedly respectable citizens, were dressed in their Sunday finest for the event. They formed a long, winding line which stretched five miles, all the way from the outskirts of Weimar, into and through the camp. The "tour" was designed to leave nothing to their imagination. They were forced to see the stacks of starved, jumbled bodies alongside the crematorium, and the bones, only half-burned, still lying inside the ovens. They saw the awful barracks where we had been kept, five to a wooden rack, all these years. And they were forced to smell the smell of Buchenwald. Of rotting human flesh and biting chlorine powder. Of the stink of 21,000 men, all eating and urinating and defecating and dying in the same small place.

Because we had been living this way for so many years, we had all acclimated to the stench and the horror of what passed for our lives. But these Germans, so neat and tidy in their dress and their habits, walked through like wax figures, barely able to understand what they were seeing.

Some of them were crying and sobbing, in sorrow and disbelief. Some of the women fainted at the sight and smell of so much horror, so much death in one place.

As the Germans filed through, in a slow, somber procession, it occurred to me that long ago this had been me and my family. My mother and my father would have looked right at home, wearing the same clothes as these people, walking the same way. I remembered that even after all these years of being beaten and starved as a Jew, I was once just a German—just like these shaken, guilt-stricken people climbing up the hill from their comfortable homes and their orderly, fastidious German lives.

Photo: United States Holocaust Memorial Museum

*The German citizens of Weimar, just a few miles from Buchenwald,
were commanded by the U.S. Army to witness the atrocities and inhuman conditions
of the camp. Dressed in their Sunday finest, they were escorted on a grisly tour of
the barracks, the gallows, the crematoria and the piles of emaciated bodies
the SS failed to burn.*

Chapter 43

Burying The Dead.

When the camp was liberated there were stacks and stacks of bodies left piled up outside the crematoria for burning. The Germans had fled before they could finish the job of disposing of all these hundreds of their victims. The bodies that had been left in our barracks, that we had been sleeping next to, had finally been hauled out into the daylight. The famous images of all these skeletal, jumbled bodies are, to many people now, the public face of Buchenwald's liberation.

A number of inmates, including those who had eaten themselves to death, had also perished since liberation day. There were still 40 or so prisoners dying every day at that point, from typhus or dysentery or simple starvation, even though everything possible was being done to save them.

The dead had been laid out, row after row, in a huge clearing. Some, who had died while the Germans were still in charge, were naked and exposed to the sky, their clothes having been stripped by the guards or even the inmates. The more recently dead still wore their tattered clothes—some the grey and blue uniforms of Jewish prisoners like me, from other camps. Some still wore the normal street clothes worn by some POWs or political prisoners.

It would be impossible to identify most of these bodies, especially since many of them had been dead for a week or more, and were decomposing rapidly, their skulls and bones starting to jut through their skin as it wasted away. There was also the problem of typhus and other diseases—something had to be done about all these rotting bodies as soon as possible. So the only thing left was to bury them in a huge mass grave.

The U.S. Army brought up its bulldozers, and they carved out a giant trench in a nearby field. The bulldozers then pushed in the bodies in one great, tumbling heap. There was no other way to do it. But it was awful.

The Americans assembled all the prisoners who wanted to attend the memorial service. I remember the huge mound of earth in front of us, where all those people who had once been alive—who had jostled with me for bread—would now rest forever.

Rabbi Schacter read the version of the Kaddish that is meant for a funeral at the gravesite of a dead Jew. The prayer says, essentially, that even though this person—in this case, hundreds of persons—were taken away in death, we still believe in God.

Photo: United States Holocaust Memorial Museum

Rabbi Schacter's memorial Kaddish service at Buchenwald. There are five boys on a bench at Rabbi Schacter's right who are facing toward the crowd. The boy in the middle, with the black hair and the German Army cap, is Henry Oster.

We stood there, and we said the words. But for me, it was simply not true.

How could a God—of all things, a Jewish God—create a world in which all these people—all these Jews, my mother, my father and 16 family members included—could be swept up and murdered, right before the eyes of the world?

How could a God have put me through the things I had survived? And then left me alone in the world with no family, no education, no money, no home and no country?

I was alive. That was about it. I didn't see very much to thank God about, frankly. If there was anyone to thank for my survival, after all those years of angst and starvation, it was me. Just this little old wise guy, all of 16 years old, Heinz Adolf Oster.

I learned later that of all the German-born Jewish children who had disappeared into the concentration camps during the war—hundreds of thousands of young Jews from Germany and other German-speaking countries—I was a member of a very exclusive club.

German-speaking Jews were mostly Germans or Austrians, of course, perhaps a few Czechs or Lithuanians, and had been rounded up in the first years of the Reich when the Nazis started their campaign of death. Which meant that of all the Jews in the camps, the German-speaking ones had, for the most part, been there longer. And thus had a much

Document: Unites States Holocaust Memorial Museum

Henry (Heinz) Oster's German SS file card recovered by the Allies from the Buchenwald concentration camp (Konzentrationslager) files. It details his birthday (November 5, 1928), home address (Brabanterstrasse 12, Koln (Cologne), his parents (Isidor and Elisabeth Oster), his detention in Lodz (called Litzmannstadt by the Germans), his detention at Auschwitz and his arrival date at Buchenwald (23.1.1945). It also shows both his identity numbers: the number on the upper right, 119497, was his prisoner number, displayed on his blue-striped prisoner jacket. The handwritten number at the top, B7648, is the number tattooed on Henry's left arm.

smaller chance of surviving.

I've been told that of all those thousands of German-Jewish boys who had been forced into the camp system, only 19 made it out alive.

Not enough to fill up a single school classroom.

Not long after our liberation, International Red Cross workers came to interview each of us, trying to understand and record who we were, where we had come from, and whether we still had any living family. I remember sitting on my bunk in the former SS barracks answering question after question in Yiddish as my interviewer wrote down the answers on his clipboard. I still have the report he made that day. It sounds strange, but it felt good to have my life set down on paper—as if I'd stopped being a human being for a time, but was now coming back into the land of the living.

Document: Unites States Holocaust Memorial Museum

Henry (Heinz) Oster's medical identity card liberated from the Buchenwald concentration camp. It shows that he was held as a political prisoner (Polit. Jude) because he was a Jew, even though he was only 12 years old when he was taken prisoner.
He had an identifying scar from an appendectomy (Blinddarmoperation) in 1936.
When he was evaluated in Buchenwald by the SS when he was 16 years old
he was just 5 feet, one inch tall (154 centimeters) and weighed just 81.4 pounds (37 kg).
By the time he was liberated by the American 3rd Army, his weight had dropped to 78 pounds.

Chapter 44

Boys In The Barracks.

As our strength and our sense of security began to grow, bit by bit, in those first few days of freedom, we started to make ourselves obnoxious the way only teenaged boys can. We were a pretty wild gang of young men at that point. We had no concept of decorum or manners. We were like a pack of lost boys who had been raised by wolves—very nasty wolves—and then suddenly thrust back into human society.

It's hard to frighten a boy after he's faced starvation, disease, brutality and, in my case, a machine-gun firing squad. We were the strong ones, the ones who had survived. Anybody weaker than us simply wouldn't have made it. So when we were crammed all together, and filled full of good GI food, we started to become a pretty testosterone-addled bunch of kids.

If we didn't like something, we yelled about it. When we weren't cramming food into our mouths, we were hiding it all over the camp. With all this new nourishment flowing into our bodies, our hormones started to assert themselves in a number of remarkable ways. I was turning from a boy into a man at a furious pace, now that my system had the extra calories to spare.

I was not the only one. Every morning in the barracks almost every boy would wake up with a proud, raging erection, ready to greet the new day. We had all spent years crammed together, five to a wooden shelf. We had been naked together, off and on, for as long as most of us could remember. There had been naked men, both dead and alive, all around us for years. So by that time we didn't feel much in the way of shame or embarrassment with each other.

We invented our own little game. While we were running around in the morning, each one of us with our proud, circumcised weiner sticking out, we decided to see whose was the strongest.

One by one, we would take a small bucket and try to hold it up, using only our raging erections. To make things more difficult—an empty bucket was not much of a challenge, really—we started to fill the bucket with water. The boy who could hold up the bucket the longest, as we filled it higher and higher with water, was the morning's champion. How did I do in this bizarre competition? Let's just say that I had my moments.

The SS and the German Shepherds were gone, but that did not mean that life in the barracks wasn't still a dangerous proposition. We were stuck there in the middle of a war zone with rough, tough soldiers and all kinds of lethal weaponry just about everywhere you looked. And like me and my young buddies back in Cologne searching for shrapnel after the air raids, we tended to poke our noses into anything that seemed cool, manly and dangerous.

We weren't the only Jews around there who were interested in weapons. A week or so after our liberation, a small group of young, serious Jewish men showed up, talking to us in Yiddish. These guys were strong and healthy—they had obviously not spent any time in the concentration camps. They were pretty secretive, but they kept asking us where they could find any guns, ammunition, or other weaponry. We later found out that these guys were Palestinian Jews and members of the Haganah, the beginnings of the Israeli guerrilla force, that was collecting weapons all over Europe for the battle they knew was coming over the founding of Israel in Palestine. We didn't have guns ourselves, but there was still no shortage of ways to get hurt.

I remember one poor kid from Vienna, one of the few German-speaking kids, who got hold of a German flare somewhere around the camp. He knew there was a small parachute inside, which was designed to let the flare float down after it had been launched in the air. We had all seen these flares in action, lighting up Auschwitz or Buchenwald whenever there was an escape or other commotion at night.

He started screwing around with this big flare, sitting there on his bunk, trying to figure out how to take it apart. He put the end of it against his body as he was wrestling with it. It went off right into his stomach. He was killed instantly, his guts sprayed all over the room in the explosion.

All for a tiny parachute.

Chapter 45

One more train ride.

After about a month and a half of increasing boredom, just hanging around Buchenwald with no real idea of what was going to happen to us, the *Oeuvre de Secours aux Enfants*, or OSE, an international Jewish organization, took over our care and prepared to transport us to the different countries that were willing to take us in, at least temporarily.

We had been forced to stay in Buchenwald for a number of reasons. First, there was still a war going on, though the combat was now happening farther and farther to the east as the Americans and the British closed the gap toward Berlin, and toward the Russian Army racing west to meet them. And second—well, the Allies really didn't know what to do with us.

We were a pretty strange group. Most of us had no families, no homes, not even a country left to go back to. We would have to be housed, fed, schooled, and then helped to find a place in a world that had been torn apart by war for six years. Not to mention the fact that there were hundreds of thousands of war refugees—the Americans called them DPs, for Displaced Persons—languishing in camps all over Europe, pushed from their homes and often their countries by the destruction of this all-engulfing conflict.

There were a total of about 1000 Jewish orphan boys still in the camp at the time. Buchenwald had become a gathering place for Jewish boys found in other camps all over Poland and Germany.

Switzerland offered to take 280 of us. England accepted 250. France took the rest of us, 427 in all. Rabbi Schacter accompanied the group that went to Switzerland and another American chaplain, Rabbi Robert Marcus, took charge of us for the trip to France.

One fine morning in early June we were told that we were leaving Buchenwald for good, and that we were going to board a train that would take us to the west. I packed up my few belongings: a change of clothes and a few bits and pieces of things, little souvenirs I had picked up around Buchenwald since our liberation.

Yet again I was herded onto a train with all the rest of my fellow Jewish orphans. I had no good idea of where we were going, where we were going to wind up, or whether things were going to get better or worse.

After all these years of being carted around like a sheep, from places that were bad to places that were worse, I had developed a severe fear of the unknown. My instinct was to stay where I was if humanly possible, because I had no idea of what I was going to face somewhere else. I would have to deal with new faces, new people, a new country and yet another new language.

I finally felt more-or-less safe here at Buchenwald for the first time in many years. I didn't want to leave. But I had no choice. None of us had a choice. The OSE was shutting down what had become our little haven at Buchenwald and the Russians were about to take over the camp. Buchenwald was in what was now becoming East Germany, under the authority of the Russians, and at least our OSE caretakers knew that we would be much better off in the West, anywhere in the West, than in the unpredictable East.

These OSE folks, mostly young Jewish men and women, were trying to help us and take care of us. They seemed, so far, to have our best interests at heart. Some of the boys were happy about this new journey we were about to take, or seemed to be putting on their best face; nobody wanted to look frightened in front of all his very male, very competitive comrades. But no matter how much the OSE people reassured me that everything was going to turn out OK, I got onto the train like a cat stepping onto a sinking boat. I was terrified.

A train had taken my family and me to Lodz. A train took my mother and me to Auschwitz. And a train had taken me—the only one of my family left—to Buchenwald. Call me crazy, but I was not so excited about getting onto another damned train. As we pulled out of the Buchenwald railroad siding—the same one I had arrived at, near death, just a few months before—I tried to look back at the place, to say good-bye in my own confused, frightened way.

My new life—the terrifying, completely unknown life that stretched before me—lay in wait on the other end of this train ride. My old life—the life of the boy who had lost just about everything a normal human possesses—was coming to an end.

The beginning of my new beginning was about to unfold. What I was looking at, craning my neck out the window at the cruel guard towers and mud and barbed wire of Buchenwald, was something else entirely. I realized that what I was seeing was the end of the end. The end of the beaten, starved, persecuted boy I had been for so many years. This was end of the stench and the hunger and the fear and the horror.

I had died in many ways, even though the mind and body of what was once called Heinz Oster were still operating: still thinking here in my head, still beating here in my heart, still breathing in my chest. I realized, as much as a 16-year-old could, that the Nazis had abused my body, but that I had never quite surrendered my self.

Photo: US Holocaust Memorial Museum

Goodbye to Buchenwald. The surviving boys were marched out of the front gate in a regimented group, like they had been so many times before under the Germans. But this time they were heading to France, and to freedom.

Chapter 46

The Ride Back To Life.

As the train gathered speed, roaring through the burned, blasted German countryside, I slowly shook off my fears and started to look forward to my new life, though I had no idea of what that life would be like.

There was plenty of food, much of it handed to us by the American GIs as we had prepared to leave the camp. We were each given a basket of provisions to last us through the train ride. I remember that there were cookies that had been given to a few of the boys, a huge basket of cookies.

The GIs had assumed that we, like any other civilized group of boys, would share the cookies among ourselves. But sharing was something we had trained ourselves not to do, over our years in the camps. If you had food in your hand you kept it, or only shared with your family or closest friends. When you don't know whether you are going to be fed tomorrow, any food you get today is the most precious thing on earth.

So we had to learn to share again. We had to finally realize that there really was going to be enough food tomorrow, and that if you gave away some of yours today, you were likely to have somebody share something of theirs tomorrow.

Because there was a shortage of good clothing in sizes suitable for the smaller boys, some of us were given leftover Hitler Youth uniforms, with the insignias removed, that the OSE had managed to scrounge somewhere in occupied Germany. So we were an odd-looking train, to be sure: rebellious, rowdy young men, seemingly taking a carefree holiday through the French countryside, dressed in the hated uniforms of the Nazis.

Some of the kids wrote messages in chalk on the side of the train. We were all slowly coming to the realization that the chances of seeing our families again were very slim. But that didn't calm down the anger that many of us felt against the Germans, and more largely against the world. How could a so-called civilized world allow what happened to us, and our brothers, our sisters, our fathers and our mothers?

One boy, a Pole from Lodz named Joe Dziubak, scrawled a sad question on the side of his train car.

"Where are our parents?" it asked in misspelled German. Hundreds of Germans, watching our train chug toward France, were forced to answer his question in their minds. In a larger sense, of course, the question was far simpler.

"What have you done, Germany? What have you done?"

The train, by then, had pretty much turned into rolling theater. We

Photo: United States Holocaust Memorial Museum

Joe Dziubak writes a question to the German people on the train leaving Buchenwald.

were traveling through a miserable, defeated Germany, and after all those years in squalor and captivity, we were now free. If anybody could be considered a winner in all this mess, we felt, for the first time in years, a little bit more like winners rather than losers.

Some of the kids wrote taunting messages: "Hitler Kaput" was one of the more popular. Some of the boys ran out and cut down branches from nearby trees when the train stopped, and waved them and shouted to anybody who would listen as we clattered through the countryside. The going was very slow. The conductor and train engineer had been

Photo: United States Holocaust Memorial Museum

On the train: From Buchenwald to Ecouis, France

told to stop and let us enjoy running free in the countryside whenever we wanted, and we wanted to stop and run around every chance we got. We were rediscovering everything. Feeling everything for the first time again. I drank in the wet grass and the wind, and inhaled the stars and the clouds rushing across the sky. Being out there, on my own, felt like running through fields of pure freedom.

Some of the boys took the opportunity to liberate anything they could get their hands on. There was a strong sense that we were entitled, in some way, to all the things we had been denied for so many years. Boys came back to the train with all kinds of treasures—mostly food, but pretty much anything was fair game. I remember one of the Hungarian kids managed to find a violin, no doubt stolen from some deserted German home, and he played it hour after hour as the train rolled on.

To the outside world we all looked pretty much the same—starved, brutalized kids with shaved heads and funny uniforms. But to us there were many differences. We were from different countries. We spoke different languages. Most of the Poles spoke Yiddish and Polish, while the Hungarians just spoke Hungarian. And we were all emotionally exhausted. We had no concept of how other people felt, or how to behave in a functioning society. We were haunted, suspicious and paranoid.

Even with all this newfound joy and freedom, there was a good deal of fighting going on, usually between Poles and Hungarians. They didn't know how to communicate with each other, and we had all been trained in the camps to take whatever we could get no matter how it might affect anybody else. So even though there was plenty of food and clothing to go around, we were still afraid, deep in our souls, that this couldn't last—that the only way to stay alive was to grab anything you could, and hang on to it for dear life.

After three days of this stop-and-go travel—the train system was still a complete mess, due to all the damage done during the fighting—we finally arrived at the border between Germany and France. I vowed to myself that I would never again set foot in Germany. I took one long, final look at the country that had betrayed me as the train rattled and screeched into France. I realized then, with a cold wave passing through me, that I was a boy without a country. I was absolutely, unquestionably alone.

Most people have a home—a place where they were raised, a familiar place to go back to for comfort, to see their old friends, their family. To rediscover who they had been, and where they had started out in life. I had nothing. Nothing at all.

There were many wonderful people who were doing their best to help us, to restore us, to make up for all the horrors we had faced, and to help us cope with what lay ahead. But you can never give back a home that has disappeared from the face of the earth, a home that simply doesn't exist anymore. You can't give back a family that has been murdered. You can't recreate a way of life after it has been smashed and burned and buried.

Yes, I was alive. But everything that I had been, almost everyone I had known, was now disappearing into the smoky haze behind our steam engine, the trail of ash and dust and cinders that trailed back behind us into Germany.

We were in France now. We were glad to be there. But the occasion was not quite as joyful an occasion as we had expected. The war-weary French civilians took one look at all these yelling, celebrating young men, hanging out of the train windows, many dressed up in recycled Hitler Youth uniforms, and assumed that we were all little Nazis, somehow being transported into France, a country the Nazis had raped and brutalized. Not knowing that we were also victims of the Nazis, the

French even tried to attack the train. We were forced to stay one night in a railroad siding outside the city of Metz to avoid the French mobs that were showing up at the various stations along the way.

The OSE leaders panicked. The last thing they wanted was for our train to be stopped, and their young charges threatened or even beaten because of a stupid misunderstanding about which uniforms we were wearing.

Photo: United States Holocaust Memorial Museum

"KL Buchenwald Waisen (orphans)." In English: "Buchenwald concentration camp orphans."

The OSE leaders quickly scrawled the words "KL Buchenwald Orphans" on the sides of the cars, to avoid confusion in the future— KL being an abbreviation of the German term *Konzentrationslager*, or "concentration camp". The message was scrawled in a mix of German and French: "*KL Buchenwald Waisen (orphans)*".

Throughout this long train ride Ivar and I stuck together as our own little fraternity. We were friends, of course, kind of a big brother and little brother, having been through so much together. And we were two of the few kids on the train who spoke German—the other boys still called us "*Yekkes*", which is Yiddish for "German". To avoid these conflicts, whenever somebody else was within earshot we tried very hard to speak Yiddish instead, to avoid raising any suspicions among our hot-headed young comrades.

As I said before, boys were getting into fights with each other because they were Polish, or Hungarian, if they found themselves with the wrong little gang on the train. We didn't need to try too hard to imagine how we would be treated if word got around that we were actually Germans.

It took another day to get from Weimar to *Les Andelys*, a beautiful little town with towering granite bluffs on the Seine river in Normandy, about 50 miles northwest of Paris. From there we were taken by a convoy of buses to *Ecouis*, another ten miles or so to the north.

Chapter 47

Welcome to the Asylum.

The OSE and the International Red Cross had arranged for us to live in the Normandy countryside. Our new home was a deserted sanatorium on an isolated estate that had been staffed by nuns before the war. The people preparing Ecouis had been told to expect a transport of 427 boys. But nobody had told them that very few younger children had survived any of the concentration camps. So instead of little boys they were faced with a bunch of angry, shaven-headed, ill-mannered teenagers.

We were housed in big dormitories with about 25 boys in a room. It was the first time I had slept on a real cot that had springs, rather than a wooden platform, ever since my family and I had been taken from our original apartment in Cologne. It doesn't sound like much now, but at the time it was a big event. It made me feel less like a prisoner, a number, a piece of material, and more like a human being.

The International Red Cross gave us some new clothing to replace the lice-infested uniforms we had been wearing. To this day, I still have two pieces of the striped camp uniform I had worn all through Auschwitz and Buchenwald.

Back in Buchenwald, I had found a German military cap which I wore because my head was still shaved. With no hair, your head gets cold pretty easily. In the famous photo of Rabbi Schacter with all the boys who were liberated at Buchenwald, there I am, with my back to the camera, with that same silly cap on my head.

I have two pictures that were taken of me in Ecouis in which I was still wearing that cap. I guess if you have nothing, the smallest things gain a certain importance. It was one thing I could hold onto, no matter where I was taken or what happened to me.

We were given wonderful food, as only the French could create. I remember that we were each given our own tin cup, and that at every meal—even breakfast—we were served wine, wonderful red French wine.

We were poor, homeless kids in a refugee orphanage. But it was France, so we couldn't have a meal without red wine. What a country. At first, we really didn't know what to do with it—this was the first alcohol we had ever tasted. It was quite a shock to go from starvation to this flood of intense new feelings and wonderful experiences.

Even though we had seen many of these other boys back in Buchenwald, we finally had the time and energy to become close friends with each other. And even though we were being fed and clothed very

Rabbi Robert Marcus, a U.S. Army chaplain, guided the 427 Buchenwald boys on their exodus from Germany to the repurposed sanatorium in Ecouis, France. Henry Oster, in his pointed German Army cap, is the boy on the left looking at the camera, directly in front of the dark-haired woman with the light-colored sweater.

well—as well as anybody could have expected—there was still a lot of anxiety. Our bodies were being taken care of, but there was still a lot of misery in our hearts. We didn't receive any counseling, per se. We just got on with our lives. This was before "post-traumatic stress syndrome" became a common psychological term, but I guess if anyone in history was prone to suffering from it, we would be the guys.

None of us knew where we would be going, or what was going to happen to us once we grew up and had to leave this island of peace and plenty. So we formed our friendships with each other, commiserating about what we were going to do with the rest of our lives. We were all waiting for some word from the Red Cross which was working overtime trying to connect all the devastated and ripped-up families the war had created, all over Europe.

Now you would do all this with computers and the internet: create a central database, and then help people find each other and connect with each other that way. But back then, everything had to be done in person, by hand-carried letters, or by mail—and this on a continent that had been bombed, starved, raped and torn apart by six years of war. I think there were well over 300,000 Holocaust survivors that the Red Cross had to house, feed, and somehow connect with each other. So for us homeless kids in Ecouis, it was a kind of slow agony, waiting for some word about our families—if we still had families. We were all waiting for someone to want us. And for many of us, that simply wasn't going to happen.

The only world we had known had disappeared. We were the few who had survived. But after a while, that didn't help ease the pain of having nobody who wanted us. Imagine knowing that nobody on the entire planet really cared about you.

At one point we were all asked to declare which country we were from—and which country we wanted to go to. I chose Palestine, a place where a refugee like me would be welcomed. I dreamed of going to America, but it seemed out of the question. My family had tried for years to get there but we never had the time, the money or the opportunity. What chance did I, a penniless kid with no education, have to make that dream come true?

Ecouis was never meant to be a permanent home for anybody. We all knew that this just a way station on the way to—well, we didn't know where it led. And late at night, alone on your cot, that's sometimes hard to take.

Teenagers are pretty high-strung and rebellious in the best of circumstances. If you wanted to create a recipe for making angry, contrary, misunderstood human beings, having your town, your country, your family and your race destroyed while the world seems to do nothing to stop it is a pretty good start.

These angry teenagers—like many teenagers, throughout human history—didn't care that the authorities, in Ecouis, were sweet people who were doing the best they could to help us. These boys knew their parents had been taken away and probably killed, and that their own lives would never be the same. The world might recover and go on. But for a shaved-headed, scrawny young Jew, with no money, no education, no family and no country, it was easy to feel that things were still pretty bleak. And to feel a lot of stored-up rage.

One by one, as time went on, a very few of the luckier boys were connected to what was left of their families, and we said good-bye to them. We were happy for them and we wished them well. But we could never be sure of what happened to them. They just disappeared, like so many of our families and friends had disappeared before.

Photo: United States Holocaust Memorial Museum

Ecouis, France: Class of 1945. Henry Oster is in the third row from the bottom, on the right, in front of the standing boy wearing a jacket with wide lapels.

Photo: United States Holocaust Memorial Museum

Henry Oster, Class Clown, Ecouis, France, 1945.

Chapter 48

Somebody from Somewhere.

For the rest of us, the Red Cross and the OSE realized that we were going to have to create our own lives for ourselves. For most of us, there was not going to be a family still alive who could bail us out.

A few of my buddies hit the jackpot and left *Ecouis* to live with distant relatives. A couple of my friends wound up going to Canada. Some went back to their country of origin, and many decided to stay in France.

For the rest of us, the assumption was that because we would eventually become French citizens because we were already in France, and France had volunteered to take us in.

This is what happened to Elie Weisel, who was another one of the boys from Block 66, in the Little Camp in Buchenwald. He was originally Romanian, but because he decided to stay there in France—which was in much better shape than Romania after the war—he became a French citizen. He also, of course, became a world-renowned writer, and the winner of the Nobel Peace Prize. I didn't know Elie by name at the time—he was just another one of the Boys from Buchenwald.

In my case, when the consul of the country of Poland came to visit Ecouis I told his staff that I was from Lodz, Poland. Of course I was not born there, but I did live there in the ghetto before I was dragged into Auschwitz and Buchenwald.

This qualified me for an identification card, similar to a passport, that showed the world that I was somebody, from somewhere. My friends, including Ivar, got their own identity papers, and this gave us a little more autonomy. It allowed us to adventure out past the gates of Ecouis and into the outside world.

The Polish Embassy also gave us each 500 French francs for spending money. All of a sudden, it seemed like I was rich.

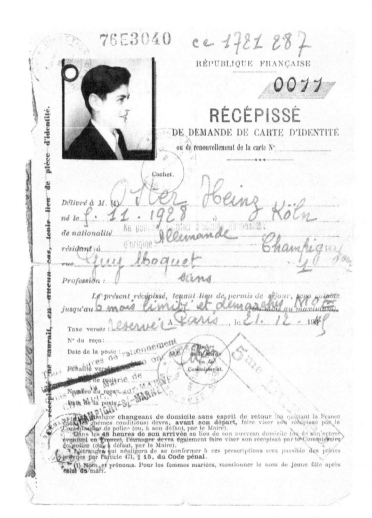

Document: Henry Oster Archive

Henry (Heinz) Oster's French ID card.

Chapter 49

What freedom looks like.

We had a lot of time to kill at Ecouis. We could only learn French
so fast, so the teachers and counselors there tried very hard to invent
useful—or at least pleasant—tasks for us, to keep us from dwelling on our
pasts or our uncertain futures.

We wound up working with our hands, doing arts and crafts with
pieces of thin plywood. We cut out silly things like windmills and little
Dutch girls with their pigtails flying up in the air. Ivar and I were pretty
much inseparable then. Neither of us had anybody else, so we became
even more like brothers.

The teachers had originally separated us boys into age groups.
That's how students are normally divided, and so that's how they were
accustomed to organizing things. The problem was that we were from so
many different backgrounds, from different countries, speaking different
languages, that there were inevitably conflicts between the various groups.
We naturally formed ourselves into what sociologists would recognize
as gangs, for companionship and support. The problem was that forcing
members of different gangs to sleep together, eat together, and go to
school together simply didn't work.

The teachers finally realized that if we were going to band into our
own natural groups, there was no good reason to stop us. So the Polish
kids stayed with the Polish kids, no matter whether they were younger
or older. The Hungarian kids grouped together. The older boys naturally
took over the role of big brothers, giving the younger kids somebody to
protect them and teach them.

We had no families. But we were forming families of our own in their
place. Ivar and I were a family. Just two scared boys who had a little in
common in our language. And everything in common, because of what
we had both been through.

There are a few other photos that have survived from our time in *Equois*, showing Ivar and me goofing around with our little wooden projects. We almost look like normal, happy young boys, with nothing better to worry about than carving wood with a little jigsaw. One day I grew tired of making what the teachers wanted me to make. It just didn't have much of a meaning after a while. Our instructor told me to make whatever I wanted. But I had no idea of what that was.

"Tell me how you felt when you were liberated," he said. I didn't understand him at first.

"Show me how it felt. What it looked like, inside."

I remembered those last, suffocating days in the barrack in Block 66, when I had to breathe through a tiny window in the top of the roof. I remembered that awful smell of rotting bodies and choking chlorine. I told the instructor that freedom meant breaking out into the open, about

Photo: United States Holocaust Memorial Museum

Henry Oster (far left behind the table) and Ivar Segalowitz (next to Henry) with their wooden sculptures at Ecouis. Henry's sculpture of his feeling of freedom, of a man in chains breaking through walls to the sun, can be seen to the right of the tall windmill.

breaking down the wall between me and the air, between me and the sun.

I made a crude wooden sculpture of a boy holding his arms out, feeling the sun and the air as a wall breaks open in front of him. I even made a yellow-painted plastic sun, shining there in the sky outside the walls.

Chapter 50

The Good Ship Exodus.

As time went on it became clear that for many of us, there was no family left to take us in and help us grow up. And like me, many of the boys didn't want to return to their home countries. If you were Polish, for instance, or Lithuanian like Ivar, there was no real point in going back. Any Jewish communities and social structures that might have existed years ago had been wiped out by the Germans. If your family had owned a house, it was likely that when you went back, there would be someone living there already who had been told the house was theirs. There was really no home to go back to.

Where did I want to go? America was my first choice, but as far as I knew I had nobody there to take me in and no way to get there. The movement to transport homeless Jews from Europe to Palestine was called *Brichah* —"flight", in Hebrew—and was gaining momentum. There were millions of Jews stuck in Displaced Person (DP) camps. After this Holocaust, the surviving Jewish people were determined to have a country of their own, so nothing like what had happened would ever happen again.

I didn't have a country to go to, so when *Brichah* representatives showed up at *Ecouis* to try to recruit Jews to come and build the country of Israel, I signed up.

I had a ticket to cross from France to Palestine on the soon-to-be-famous ship, The Exodus 1947, which was destined to be the scene of a battle between Jews who wanted to go to Palestine against the British authorities who were, at the time, in charge of the place. The British didn't want to let in a flood of Jewish refugees, most without legal immigration certificates. And the Arabs and Palestinians who lived there in Palestine were not so excited about the idea either.

But the *Haganah*, the military wing of the movement to create Israel, wanted to force the world to see the injustice Jews were still suffering.

So they were preparing to run this old second-hand ship from France to Israel, challenging the British to stop them with force, and show the world yet another scene of Jews being pushed around and persecuted.

So it looked like at some point in the near future I was going to be a citizen of Israel—if only I could get there in one piece and not be beaten or jailed by the British or set upon by the Arabs.

As our time dragged on there, the *Ecouis* authorities also decided that if we were going to be stuck there much longer we were going to need a profession, and began to give us the education we would need to succeed. What did I want to be? To begin my education, I had to decide what it was that I wanted to do for the rest of my life. What I really wanted to do was to be a comedian.

Throughout all the hopeless situations and craziness I went through, I had always seemed to be the one who would try to lighten the mood—to make something a little funny out of any situation. When everyone around you is in a terminal depression, a state of constant pessimism—in our friends' and family's case, for some very good reasons—it's not that hard to be the funniest guy in the room. Of course, a lot of my humor had to do with one simple fact: I didn't know any better. I didn't know how bad things really were.

People would tell me: "You're so damned funny. You should be a comedian." And after enough of this, over the years, I started to believe them. Of course, I didn't really have any real talent or ability in that direction. It's one thing to make your friends and family laugh, but it's quite another to get up in front of a room full of strangers and make them laugh, every time, day in and day out.

And the teachers at *Ecouis*—like most smart teachers and parents around the world—were not so sure that being a comedian was going to work out as a practical career for me. It wasn't my first choice, but I started to train to become a civil engineer, the people who design and build bridges and roads and tunnels. I was not so crazy about the idea.

It didn't seem like it would be nearly as much fun as hanging out in cabarets and nightclubs, making everybody laugh while the girls admired me from the back of the room. Or at least that was how the fantasy went.

Unlike many of the boys, I did know how to read and write. In German, of course, and in Hebrew, from when I had been studying for my clandestine Bar Mitzvah, but certainly not in French. So I had a lot of work cut out for me.

So I went to civil engineering school. For exactly one day.

Chapter 51

The Man From America.

When I came home from engineering school in the afternoon there was a gentleman waiting for me, a civilian. He introduced himself and told me that he was the vice-consul of the United States, from the American embassy in Paris.

He told me, in French I could barely understand, that after the Red Cross took all the information from me back in Buchenwald—the names and addresses of all the relatives I could remember—they had found a connection.

They had taken my uncle's name—Herbert Haas, one of my mother's brothers—and had investigated my recollection that he had lived in Philadelphia.

"I have to tell you," he said, "Your uncle Herbert doesn't live in Philadelphia now. But nevertheless, he found your name in a newspaper in Los Angeles.

"The Red Cross has been asking newspapers around the world to publish the names of survivors like you. In Los Angeles, way out in California, there's a Jewish newspaper called *B'nai B'rith*, which means 'The Truth' in Hebrew.

"Your uncle found your name in that newspaper. And he is willing to let you become part of his family—he is offering to have you come to the United States to live with him and his wife."

It was a moment that changed my life. It began my life, really. I exploded with joy. Somebody, somewhere out there, wanted me. After years of being abandoned by nearly everybody, and every institution I had encountered, I couldn't believe that now this was happening. When the entire world seems to turn its back on you, for all those years, you start to feel, somehow, like you don't really deserve to be treated like a human being. After all these years of being broken down, of being made to feel worthless, now this.

I was crazy with happiness. But I really had no idea of what this all really meant. Who would think that after all this, I would wind up going to America—a country of sheer fantasy, the country where nearly everybody in the world wanted to live. It was a miracle, like so many others over the years, that happened to me.

My plans to go to Palestine were scrapped that afternoon. I had no interest in going to what might be another long war, with both the British and the Palestinians, when instead I could go to America. I wound up giving my ticket on the Exodus to another friend at *Ecouis*.

Even though I now had this idea of where I was going, I still had to figure out how I was going to get there. There were no civilian passenger ships going from France to America this soon after the war. Every available ship was filled with American and Canadian troops going home.

And even if there had been a ship to sail on, how was a penniless Jewish orphan going to pay for the trip? I had no money, and neither did my uncle Herbert and my aunt Bertha. It would still be months before I could think of getting to the U.S.

Chapter 52

A Free Man In Paris.

As many of the boys found other places to live, *Ecouis* was eventually shut down and different groups of the Boys of Buchenwald were sent to other facilities in France.

Of all places I wound up at an estate owned by the Rothschilds, which was at one time the richest family in the Western world. They had volunteered to have a group of orphans stay at one of their many estates all over Europe.

This sounded great until we got there. It turned out that instead of living in splendor in one of the Rothschilds' mansions we were shoveled into the servants' quarters, hidden in the rear of the place where the guests and family would never go.

The servants' quarters were dirty and falling apart. And when you hear that from somebody who has survived Auschwitz, you can believe it. I wound up contracting scabies from the dirty beds and linens. It's a mite that penetrates the skin and multiplies underneath, and it's about the most awful, itchiest thing you can imagine. I had this so bad that I had to be taken to a hospital in Paris to have it treated.

But even this wound up turning out in my favor, though it would have been hard to convince me of that at the time. The treatment consisted of a burning, toxic bath I had to take twice a day. It turned my skin purple: I looked like a Smurf every time I had to go through it.

The good news was that I met a lovely French nurse named Carmen during my treatment. She was one of the women who helped bathe me, so I guess you could say that I didn't have any secrets from her. When I was cured—and I wasn't purple all over any more—I was discharged from the hospital and transferred to a new home in *Champigny-sur-Marne*, on the southeast outskirts of Paris.

In the packets that my uncle had been sending to me there were always two cartons of cigarettes. Which was a great thing, because even though I didn't smoke—I almost passed out again when I tried—these cigarettes were like cash in those days of deprivation and rationing. So I had a little extra cash in my pocket, so I could go out on the town a little bit and be able to afford a few little things. And my new friend Carmen— well, she was a smoker, so having cigarettes probably made me a little bit more attractive than I might have seemed otherwise.

I kept in contact with Carmen, of course, and one night, after we saw a movie, she invited me to up to her room in the nurses' dormitory. She was very sweet. She was proud of her skill with the violin, and she insisted on playing for me. Before I knew it she had put down the violin, turned out the lights and took me to bed. We made love, I for the first time in my life. She was very kind and patient and understanding. It was a wonderful introduction to the world of sexual pleasure, and quite a contrast to where I had been, and what I had gone through. A few months before, I had been starving in Buchenwald. Now I was larking about Paris with a bit of money in my pocket, and I was even sleeping with my own French girlfriend.

Even now, I still joke that whenever I hear a violin playing, I can feel something stirring in my pants.

The other boys from *Champigny-sur-Marne* and I loved to wander all over Paris. It was like being in heaven. Many of the most sought-after Parisian attractions, like the shows at the *Folies Bergére* and the *Moulin Rouge*, were free to us. We were given this wonderful green pass that said, in French, "Extend any Courtesy to Veterans and Ex-Prisoners."

It was at the *Folies Bergére* that I saw a naked woman for the first time in my life—my adventures with Carmen had all taken place in the warm, sweet darkness of her dormitory room.

My pals and I could go to the theaters and shows any time we wanted. It was almost too good to be true. Drinking wine and watching beautiful French dancers was a lovely introduction to the pleasures of life in the free world.

One night some friends and I took the train to *Pigalle*, the famous theater- and red-light district of the city, to see a movie double feature. I remember it was *Gunga Din* with Cary Grant, Douglas Fairbanks Junior and Sam Jaffe, a nice Jewish boy, in the title role as a miserable Indian water bearer. We also saw *The Four Feathers*, another movie about the British military making trouble in a foreign country, starring C. Aubrey Smith.

When the movie was over our little gang spilled out into the streets, soaking in all the lights and sounds and uninhibited life going on around us. We weren't there to find prostitutes—at least not to avail ourselves of their services. We really didn't know what a prostitute was. We were so clueless and wet behind the ears, we just knew that they were supposed to be bad women.

Photo: Henry Oster Archive

Henry Oster and Ivar Segalowitz, Paris, 1945.

But boys—especially horny young ex-prisoners—will watch girls, and that's just what we did.

One French girl sidled up to me and in a very sexy voice made what one might call an indecent proposition. I was startled and flustered, and mostly out of shock and surprise, I called her the French word I had learned for whore. Which, I soon learned, also meant "pig." I soon found out that Paris is a city that takes its prostitution very seriously. These girls were respected in their profession, licensed by the city, and protected by the law and by the police far more than in most other places. This woman took great offense at what I had blurted out and started screaming. The next thing I knew I was in the hands of the *Gendarmes*, who dragged me off to the local police station, protesting all the way in bad French. Believe me, the last thing I wanted was to find myself a prisoner again.

Leave it to me to get myself thrown in jail for just walking down the street, and saying the wrong word to a hooker. There was a big commotion, with my friends following me to the police station to try to get me out. The fine was 200 francs—200 francs that I didn't have. I was trying to explain how sorry I was, that I didn't speak French, and that I had meant no disrespect to the fine young woman who had so graciously offered me her favors.

In consideration for my youth, my status as an Auschwitz and Buchenwald survivor, and my obvious lack of skill in the language, the fine was reduced to 100 francs, which the people running our home and I finally scraped together. When we made it out of the door and down the steps of the station, now in the small hours of the morning, there was the prostitute I had insulted, waiting for us. She was weeping at the trouble she had gotten me into—once she knew my circumstances, she felt awful about having made such a big deal out of my dumb mistake. She even gave me back 50 francs of her own, to make up for what I had been through.

Photo: Henry Oster Archive

Another French ID card, denoting Henry Oster's stay in Lodz, Poland and his liberation from Buchenwald on April 11, 1945.

Photo: Henry Oster Archive

Henry Oster and Ivar Segalowitz, Paris, 1945

Chapter 53

To The Promised Land.

On another, happier day Ivar, a couple other friends and I went strolling up the magnificent *Avenue des Champs-Élysées*, the broad, light-filled boulevard that ends at the *Arc de Triomphe*, the famous arch at the top of the long hill. We stopped to have coffee and something sweet at one of the many cafés along the avenue. And while we were there, chattering away in German and Yiddish, depending on who was talking, the waiter came up and spoke to us.

"Pardon me," he said. "Please excuse the interruption, but there is a gentleman a few tables over who heard you speaking German, and who would like to meet you young men." We were introduced to Mr. and Mrs. Rosenthal, a German Jewish couple who had escaped from Nazi Germany to France in 1937, and who had managed to hide there from the Germans throughout the war.

He told us that he had taken a job in the French Ministry of Transportation. And that now, of all the people in France we could have met, he was the French Minister of Transportation.

If there was anybody who could help me get out of France and over the Atlantic to America, this was the guy. After our meeting at the café Mr. Rosenthal and his wife adopted me in a way, and for the next few weeks I went over to their house in Paris for Friday dinners, getting to know them and their family. As time went by, a plan was hatched to get me over the Atlantic.

It turned out that Mr. Rosenthal had a brother who lived in Los Feliz, a nice palm-tree-lined neighborhood in the north-central part of Los Angeles, California. And that Mr. Rosenthal had been looking for a way to send money to his brother, but without the red tape and expense of officially sending it to him from France.

Mr. Rosenthal proposed that my uncle, who was already in Los

Angeles, give the money for my ship fare to his brother in Los Feliz, and that then he would buy me the ticket for my ship's passage to the States here in Paris.

He also pulled some strings and booked my passage on the *Desiré*, a rust-bucket freighter that was going from Normandy all the way to New York. This was the first ship that was carrying civilians from France to New York after the war. And now I, of all the refugees in Europe, had a

Photo: Henry Oster Archive

Henry's French passport document, detailing his mother's death in Auschwitz and his emigration to live with his uncle in Los Angeles.

golden ticket to be on it.

I said goodbye to Ivar. I had no idea of whether or not I would ever see him again. He was sad to see me go, and I imagine it must have been terrifying to him to lose yet another part of his past, and to say goodbye to the big brother who had tried to look after him ever since Buchenwald.

But we both knew I had to go. There was no question about it. Ivar was in good hands there, quickly learning French and getting a good education in Paris. I had a family and maybe a good new life an ocean away. So I was off.

I said goodbye to all my other friends and teachers and boarded a train in Paris headed for the port of Cherbourg. Paris had been spared from destruction during the war, but Cherbourg, which was the nearest port to the D-Day landings in Normandy, had been battered by the Allies from the air, from the sea and on the ground, and there were remnants and relics of war everywhere. When the ship left Cherbourg Harbor we were dodging leftover German mines. The crew even shot at some, trying to explode them before they could explode us. None of them went off, and we were soon on the open Atlantic, thumping along with a trail of black oil smoke, bound on a two-week-long voyage to New York City.

Chapter 54

The Woman in the Harbor.

When you arrive in New York on a broken-down ship and you see the Statue of Liberty: well, it's an experience that's almost impossible to describe. I don't care how many people have tried to say it, but when you see that impossible statue, with that torch held up in the air, everything changes.

The concept of what you are, who you are, what you have been through—it changes completely at just that moment. That incredible, beautiful, symbolic structure tells you that you have arrived at the gate of something that your imagination could not possibly conceive.

People who are born in America have no way of understanding what America means to poor, beaten-up, desperate people who have run out of luck or money or space in whatever country they came from. To these people—people like me, that grey day in April 1946—America is much more than a new place. It is a new life.

I had almost no money. I spoke no English. I had no skills. I had no home, and no real family. But even to me, coming here with nothing, it felt like I was the luckiest kid on earth. After all those years of being despised and nearly annihilated by the Nazis, having so many things go right in my life seemed like a long, wonderful dream. It's a dream I have still not awakened from, all these years later.

I stayed for a short time in New York with a distant relative, Millie Lachman, who was a cousin of my mother, and her husband Henry, whom I had known in Germany. I also reconnected with a couple friends I had known in Cologne. One was a boy about my age who was the son of one of my mother's cousins, and another was an old classmate of mine, from way back in 1935 before the Germans had kicked us out of school.

These wonderful people showed me my first glimpses of America.

I was nearly knocked over by the sight of my first American

supermarket. There was nothing like this in Europe. Everybody there bought their groceries at a local store, within walking distance of their homes. Here was a cathedral dedicated to food in its every incarnation. Walls of bread. Oceans of milk. A meat counter bigger than any home I had ever lived in. Fresh, glowing-green vegetables and rainbows of fruit from every corner of the world.

The Automat was another American invention that took my breath away. It seems a little spooky and industrial now, but at the time it was an astounding invention. You put your 50 cents into a slot, and then reached in to a revolving machine to grab the sandwich you wanted. It was robotic and machinelike, but it was also hip and modern and fast. You could get a sandwich in a few seconds—no more waiting for an actual person to take your order, put your meal together, and then take your money and make change. Bang, bang, bang, things happened here in America faster than anywhere else on earth.

All this food was a visual treat, and an eye-opening look at a whole new world, the world of the future, spread out right before my dazzled eyes. But in an odd way, the food itself really didn't excite me.

Even now, once people meet me and realize what I went through all those years ago, they seem to have an unreasoning need to feed me. "You were starving," they will say. "You need to eat more."

I hate to disappoint these well-meaning people, but food really doesn't mean much to me. It hasn't since I left Buchenwald. That was then, and this is now. I can't make up now for what I couldn't eat then. It may be that my stomach, and my metabolism, grew up with next to nothing to eat, and that it never changed after I came to America, the capital of too-much-to-eat. I don't have any desire to eat much at a time, and sometimes it seems like such a chore, eating and cleaning up and digesting, that I wish I didn't have to do it at all.

Photo: *Henry Oster Archive*

Henry Oster, New York, 1946

Chapter 55

Home at Last.

When I got to Los Angeles, my Uncle Herbert and Aunt Bertha were sincerely glad to see me, to adopt me and to help me create a life here in America.

But it was easy to see in their eyes that they pitied me as well. I was a scrawny, pathetic-looking creature, at least in comparison to all the healthy, milk-fed people of Los Angeles. People would tell me: "You're so pale! You're so thin!" Well, I was looking fantastic, compared to how I had looked just months before.

I had been a tiny bit taller than most of the other boys at the beginning, but now my body was doing everything it could to catch up. Once I came to California and began to live a more normal life, my body sprouted like a sunflower plant. I grew four inches in one year.

I remember my aunt and uncle buying me my very first complete suit. I was very proud of it. But I never got to wear it in public. By the time a family wedding came up that required me to put it on, my arms were poking way out of the sleeves like the wooden arms of a scarecrow.

I was glad that I was growing, but it was painful. My joints were sore all the time. They were undergoing the growing pains of those lost years, all in few short months. My body felt like it didn't fit me anymore.

My aunt and uncle couldn't have been more loving or more welcoming. In retrospect, it seemed that because they had not been prepared to have children of their own, because of all the hardships they had suffered, they poured all those years of wanting to be parents into me. They tried to spoil me, I guess. Some of my friends and present family might think that they succeeded.

Back in Philadelphia my aunt had been forced to do piecework in a clothing factory to make ends meet, making uniform coats for American soldiers.

My Uncle Herbert, like the rest of us German Jews, had not been able to get any kind of an education before he left for America. But he loved cars. He had raced cars back in Germany, and he had been injured in a racing crash when he was young. He had an enormous scar on his cheek from that accident that he wore all his life.

The only work he could get, back in Germany in the 30s, was as a salesman for Opel, which is now the German subsidiary of General Motors. Then he met his wife, my Aunt Bertha, and moved to my home city of Cologne. The only job he could get—as a Jew, of course, he was not allowed to own his own business—was in a garage, working on other people's automobiles. When he came to America he did the same thing. He ran an Atlantic Richfield gas station—the company now known as ARCO—on Wilshire Boulevard in downtown L.A., right next to Good Samaritan Hospital.

He was working there at his gas station when a gentleman who happened to be the owner of the *B'nai B'rith Messenger*, a famous old Jewish paper in Los Angeles, stopped by. This guy was a longtime customer of my Uncle Herbert's filling station, and he knew that Herbert was trying to find any members of his family who had survived the insanity in Europe.

Every Friday, when the paper was published, he would make sure to stop by my uncle's gas station on the way home, fill up with Atlantic Richfield gas, and give my uncle a free copy of the paper.

That's how my uncle discovered that I was still alive: the wild chance of a publisher dropping off a certain paper, on a certain Friday, that had my name on a list of concentration-camp survivors.

I quickly learned when I got to L.A. that running a gas station was not a great way to make a living. My uncle was not the owner—operators like him had to lease their stations from the oil companies. Atlantic Richfield controlled everything.

Uncle Herbert only made 3 or 4 cents per gallon of gasoline. He could only sell Pennzoil oil, and he could only sell Goodyear tires. The only way he could make some extra money was to do service on his customer's cars: repairs, oil changes, chassis lubrication, tires, wiper blades and brake-shoe replacements. That money, for his labor and the small profit on the parts, was his to keep.

Uncle Herbert's station was not in a good location. It was on Wilshire Boulevard, a well-traveled street in this huge, bustling city. But it was not where a lot of people lived, so people were rushing by on their way

to work and back when they passed his station, and were not inclined to
stop and get their cars serviced there.

It was tough going. My new adoptive parents had been forced to
borrow money to post a bond for me, to show the government that they
had enough resources to care for me, so I wouldn't be a burden on the
system here. So they had to pay that money back, month by month, in
addition to what it actually cost us to live.

My Uncle Herbert and Aunt Bertie lived in a rented house in
Hollywood, a tiny little one-floor California Bungalow. They had only
one bedroom. So just as before, in my travels, I had to sleep in the living
room. They pulled out a folding sofa bed for me.

And that's where I slept every night from 1946 well into the 50s.
Of course I had to go to school. And since I hadn't been to school since
1935, I had a lot of catching up to do. For starters, I didn't speak a word of
English. German, yes. Yiddish, yes. A little Polish. But nothing in English
more complicated than "hello" and "goodbye."

There were thousands of kids coming in to the city after the war,
displaced people from all over the world who now had to be educated
here in Los Angeles. To make thing simpler for everybody, all of us
new foreign kids—none of whom spoke English—were assigned to go
to Belmont High School. There we could get three hours of English
instruction every day, instead of the usual one-hour class, so we had a
fighting chance of catching up to all these native California students.

From our bungalow in Hollywood I had to take the streetcar down
Beverly Boulevard to high school every morning. And by a stroke of luck,
the school was about 5 or 6 blocks away from my uncle's service station.

Every day after school I walked to the station and went to work, from
3:30 in the afternoon to midnight. My uncle trained me in running the
station, selling the gas and keeping the accounts, as well as doing some
of the simpler repairs and service for his customer's cars. He would come
and pick me up every night when my shift was done. Sometimes he would
come early and stay with me after dinner and keep me company, so I
could do my homework there in the gas-station office.

This let him save the money he would have spent on hiring another
person to run the station when he wasn't there, so at least I had a chance
to enrich their lives a little—to repay my aunt and uncle for the amazing
love and support they were giving me. It felt good to know that I was
making a contribution, for all the sacrifices they had made to take me in
and raise me, and for the money they had spent to give me a new life.

After a few years, Uncle Herbert had saved enough money so we could move to a bigger, nicer place, up on Genesee Street in Hollywood. I got my own bedroom, and my own, personal bed with a wooden frame, a spring base, a mattress and everything. It was the first time I had my own real, authentic bed since 1935. It seems like a tiny thing, but it meant a lot to me at the time. I was now a real person who deserved a real bed just like everybody else.

That's how I lived for ten years, working in my uncle's gas station every night, through high school and all the way through college. It took ten years to transform myself from a homeless, skinny German Jewish refugee into a Californian. My aunt had been adamant that I needed to work hard, go to a good college, and find a profession where I could use my brain. She wasn't going to let me miss out on the opportunity I had been given, by coming here to America and to California.

"If you have come this far, and survived all the things you have, you have to do something special with the gifts you have been given," she told me.

She didn't want me to wind up like my uncle, wonderful man that he was, in having to scratch a living out of oil changes and tire rotations, coming home every night with axle grease and dirty oil under his fingernails.

She didn't have to work too hard to convince me. Where a lot of the boys I went to high school with got distracted with getting their own cars, chasing girls, drinking beer and screwing around, I took things a little more seriously. Many of the boys I knew—mostly other European Jewish survivors who had come to California after the war like me—seemed to get themselves bogged down.

They weren't as interested in their schoolwork and building their futures as I was. And I guess you can't blame them. They had come from so little and had come here with, in many cases, less than nothing. They wanted to live their lives right then, at full throttle. They wanted to have fun, and run a little crazy, and have girlfriends; maybe get married and even have kids.

After all the craziness I had been through I guess I was dedicated to being the master of my own destiny from then on. The way I saw it I'd already been poor and starved and subjected to the whims of some very evil people. From now on, I wanted to be in charge of my own life. If I had anything to do about it, I wanted this story to have a happy ending.

I was in a hurry. I graduated from Belmont High—which is still there today—in two and a half years, partly because I had shown up in the middle of the first school year, back in 1946. I graduated in the top 3% of my class. Of course, it didn't hurt that I was 18 years old when I started, instead of the usual 14 or 15. I was already 21 when I graduated. So I was a lot more mature than most of the other kids in my classes. I also concentrated pretty hard. I gave up some of the social niceties that distracted some of my buddies at Belmont High. But now that I had achieved this—learning English, and graduating from high school with good grades—what the heck was I going to do with the rest of my life?

Photo: Henry Oster Archive

Henry Oster, Aunt Bertha Haas and Uncle Herbert Haas, Los Angeles, 1946

Chapter 56

Welcome to Westwood.

I decided to go to college at UCLA—or, rather, my circumstances decided for me. We still didn't have much money, so I needed to go to college somewhere nearby so I could continue to live with my aunt and uncle, and so I could keep on working at my uncle's gas station. He needed me there, and it was the only way I knew to make a little money to finance my college career.

UCLA was relatively inexpensive, unlike some of the more-exclusive, more-prestigious private colleges in the city like USC. And UCLA was very welcoming of foreign students, from all races and backgrounds. People came from all over the world to go to UCLA, just as they do today. There were a lot of Jewish kids, like me—refugees and survivors—so I would have no trouble finding friends with whom I would have a lot in common.

But what did I want to be? I still had it in the back of mind that I wanted to be a comedian, but that wasn't really a realistic goal. I spoke with a German accent, which isn't a great base for comedic material after World War II. And my background—well, talking about my experiences as a Holocaust survivor didn't seem to be a sure-fire way to get laughs night after night.

At the time I was spending a lot of time going to the dentist. The malnutrition I had been through had screwed up the development of my teeth. My teeth and my gums just weren't the same size, so initially it looked as if I was likely to wind up with dentures instead of my own teeth.

But I found a great dentist who took me on as a challenge. I went two or three times a week, getting my teeth rehabilitated as best as I could. My teeth turned out well in the end—I still have them, in other words, 68 years later. My dentist and I got to know each other very well, and it seemed like an interesting way to make a living. So I decided to follow a

Pre-Med preparation for dental school at UCLA, getting the education and credentials I would need to enter dental school.

Somewhere along the way I got my first car, a very used 1936 Ford Sedan with a soft top. It wasn't a convertible, but it had a cloth roof instead of a steel one. The goofy top leaked so badly, it poured water on my head, my papers and my books every time it rained.

My uncle had lots of opportunities to buy used cars at good prices—customers were often coming in trying to get rid of the cars they had, in order to afford a better, newer one. So before long, we sold the Ford and got a cool little '39 Chevy convertible, a blue one that even matched the UCLA school colors.

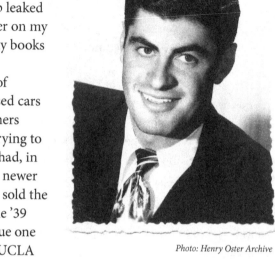

Photo: Henry Oster Archive

High School Graduation, Belmont High

When I wasn't going to college, I was working at the gas station. Except for Saturday afternoons. That was when my uncle would hire a part-time worker to run the station so I could go to the UCLA football games, just like every other carefree, fun-crazy American student.

My friends and I really got into the spirit of the thing. We dressed my Chevy up in blue and yellow flags and ribbons and pom poms. We blasted through the streets of Westwood and all over the campus, honking the horn and screaming whenever UCLA won a game.

It seems silly and childish now, and it was. But I figured I had earned the right to be a little childish now and again. Most of the UCLA students around me had enjoyed safe, secure childhoods. Most of them had parents back home and entire families who had supported them all their lives. I had never had a childhood. So I had to pick up little scraps of one, day by day, as I grew from a skinny, awkward teenager with halting English and bad teeth into a full-grown American man.

UCLA was not easy for me. I was told by one English teacher to present myself in his office because, he said, "I cannot pass you with the kind of mistakes you are making with the language."

He had been making so many red marks on my papers, they looked like red-and-white barber's poles when he handed them back. I tried to

Photo: Henry Oster Archive

Henry Oster and Herbert Haas, at Uncle Herbert's Atlantic Richfield station, Wilshire Boulevard, Los Angeles.

explain, but he cut me off.

"You speak with an accent. Weren't you born here?" he asked me.

"No," I said, I've only been here since 1946".

"Why didn't you tell me this?" he asked. "You can't learn English as a second language that fast, when all these other kids have been speaking it from the day they were born."

So he agreed to give me some special attention, and to adjust my grade a little, considering the short time I had even heard, let alone spoken, this new language.

I had unofficially changed my name from my original name, Heinz Adolf Oster, to the more American Henry Oster when I first arrived in New York in 1946.

First of all, I didn't want to be known as a ketchup, and whenever an American says "Heinz", that's all they can think of. Henry is simply the English version of Heinz.

My Grandfather—my father's father—had been named Adolf, and that's how it got to be my middle name. I had been swatted more than once by Nazis who didn't appreciate that my official name according to them—Heinz Adolf Israel Oster—had "Adolf" and "Israel" so close together. That was easy to drop. So in 1951, as I started at UCLA, I became a U.S. citizen. Henry Oster, All-American college guy.

UCLA was just as tough as high school. I was still working 40 hours a week in my uncle's gas station, which was now a Mobil station on Selma Avenue and Vine Street, just a block south of the famous corner at Hollywood and Vine.

UCLA was challenging, but it was fair. I never got the impression that I was ever discriminated against because I was from a foreign country, that I had a German accent, or that I was Jewish. It was a wonderful school with a positive, tolerant attitude, a very diverse and interesting faculty and student body, and I had every opportunity I could have wished for.

Because I was three years older than most of the other students, and because now I had to shave every morning, a few of the girls I went to school with saw me as a little bit sexier than the other guys. I had more of a mysterious, Continental vibe going on, I guess you could say. But I really didn't have time go mess around with romantic stuff, or even go to the movies. I pretty much had my head down, working like crazy to get where I wanted to go in life.

And my new family never had enough money to go out and do much, other than stay home and go to work. At one point I was able to save enough money to take my adoptive parents down to San Diego to stay at the Coronado Hotel. And I also took them on a trip to Lake Tahoe, in the mountains on the border between California and Nevada. But these were very rare, very special occasions.

All in all, nevertheless, I was as grateful as hell to be here. I was going to college in California, of all places, one of the nicest places in America—right where everybody else in the world wanted to be. After so many years of everything going wrong, it seemed as if now they were always going right.

UCLA 1954

Henry Oster, American citizen, and medium-sized man on campus.

Chapter 57

Sorry. Too Jewish.

When I graduated from UCLA, I decided I wanted to go to the School of Dentistry at USC—the University of Southern California.

Which was a hard decision to make, as a dyed-in-the-wool UCLA student. UCLA and USC are legendary cross-town rivals, and winning the annual football game between the two schools is enough to create bragging rights for an entire school year.

But UCLA didn't have a school of dentistry. The closest California public school with a strong dentistry program was the University of California at Berkeley, all the way up north near Oakland.

USC, on the other hand, was close enough to Hollywood so I could continue to live with my Aunt Bertha and Uncle Herbert, and the tuition was low enough so I had a fighting chance of being able to afford it. So I prepared myself to go there.

I gathered the transcript of my UCLA grades and applied to USC. I passed every test I needed to qualify.

In one test I had to carve a sculpture from of a piece of chalk, to show the examiners that I had the manual dexterity I would need to be a good dentist. When I handed the little chalk figure in to the examiner, for him to carefully wrap it and pack it, the knucklehead promptly dropped it on the floor, dashing it into pieces. He was very apologetic, and made sure to make a note that he had dropped my work of art, and that it was fine before he got his clumsy hands on it.

Things looked good at first. I was treated with all kinds of courtesy, and was granted an interview with the chairman of the admissions committee, a certain Dr. Rutherford.

Before the interview, I spoke to our family friend, the guy who was the owner of the *B'nai B'rith Messenger*, the Jewish newspaper that had originally alerted my uncle that I was still alive in France after the war.

One day, as he stopped by our service station, he told me that gaining admission to USC was going to be difficult, because of all the veterans from World War ll and the Korean war who had preference when they came back out of the service.

But he had a plan. He said, "If you could make an "endowment"— that is, a gift of money or property—"at the same time you submit your application, you will be assured of getting in."

Well, we had no money at all. I was going to college and working in a gas station, for crying out loud. He made some inquiries at USC: "I tell you what you do," he said, "You can buy a television set, and donate it as a gift to this gentleman, Dr. Rutherford, the chairman of the admissions committee. It might help your chances of getting in."

Well, a television was a very new and expensive thing then. I didn't have one—it would be years before I could afford one for myself. It cost about as much then as it does now: I bought one for about $250, about what you would pay in WalMart today for a small flat-screen. But due to inflation, the dollar was worth about ten times as much back then as it is today. So in today's dollars, I had to pay nearly $2500. And believe me, that was $2500 I didn't have to spare.

Nevertheless, gritting my teeth, I sent off this brand-new TV—a television was a rare and wonderful thing back then, kind of like the radio my family had owned in back in 1933—to this Dr. Rutherford. And never heard anything about it. There was no acknowledgment that it had arrived, no hint that it had been appreciated.

When the day finally came for my interview, Dr. Rutherford told me, "You know, I'm sure you have heard it through the grapevine that we rarely accept anybody the first year they apply—we have so many students backlogged. But since you have already applied and fulfilled all the requirements, we will leave your name on the list of applicants. We'll leave it in the hopper. So you won't have to go through the process again. You will hear from us. We'll go ahead and consider you again next year, but with the advantage that you will already be that much farther up the list, so you'll have a much better chance of being accepted then."

At one point in the interview Dr. Rutherford got up and excused himself to attend to another matter. I took a peek at my application papers, sitting there on his desk. And written across the top of the cover were the words: "Germ Jew." "German Jew", in other words.

I had a bad feeling about that.

I hadn't given it much thought at the time—I had been treated so fairly everywhere in America, and all the way through high school and college in California, that I had started to forget that anti-Semitism was still a problem. In other words, I was pretty naive.

USC was originally a Methodist Christian college, and had a long-standing reputation of not accepting Jews. The word was that before the war, USC had a very specific *numerous clausus*, or quota program: Each year, one Jewish student was admitted to the medical school, one to the dental school, and one to the law school.

I didn't know that the President of USC until 1947, Rufus Bernhard von KleinSmid, had been a co-founder of the Human Betterment Association. This group advocated the bizarre Eugenics and forced-sterilization policies that the Nazis used as a "scientific" rationale for segregating, sterilizing, and finally exterminating the mentally ill, homosexuals and Gypsies. Not to mention millions of Russians and six million of my own Jewish people, including most of my family and very nearly myself.

The twisted theories of von KleinSmid and his colleagues influenced more than 30 states, including California, to legalize the forced sterilization of the "feebleminded and the insane." As I detailed earlier over 60,000 people were sterilized under these laws, a third of them in California.

"The application of the principles of Eugenics to organized society is one of the most important duties of the social scientist of the present generation," wrote von KleinSmid in a 1913 paper presented to the Cincinnati Academy of Science: "We must all agree that those who, in the nature of the case, can do little else than pass on to their offsprings (sic.) the defects which make themselves burdens to society, have no ethical right to parenthood."

To this day, the USC website contains an historic timeline http://about.usc.edu/history that includes Doctor von KleinSmid, "affectionately known as Dr. Von," becoming the University President in 1921. He held that post until 1947, just six years before I applied to USC's School of Dentistry.

To be fair, von KleinSmid was not alone in his misguided—and ultimately genocidal—theories. David Starr Jordan, Stanford University's first president, the *Los Angeles Times* publisher Harry Chandler, and Nobel-Prize-winning physicist Robert A. Millikan were also members of the Eugenics-obsessed Human Betterment Association. And as I wrote earlier in the book, these contagious ideas of some people being inherently inferior to others were used by Adolf Hitler to give a pseudo-scientific basis to his efforts to murder millions of innocent human beings.

But I didn't know this when I was trying to get into USC's dentistry program. All I knew was what Dr. Rutherford had told me—that I would be favorably considered for admission the next year.

Around July of that year, I started to worry a bit. Acceptances for admission to the Dentistry School usually went out in May or June, but here it was the summer already, and I had not heard from them.

I made another appointment with Dr. Rutherford. And it quickly became clear that he had no intention of admitting me, no matter what he had said the previous year. He looked me in the eye and said to me, "Well, Henry, you didn't make another application."

I said, "No, because I actually trusted you. You said you would leave me "in the hopper" with last year's applicants."

"Well," he said. "You should have still made a new application."

I knew I was screwed. I was angry beyond words, and dejected. I had worked so hard, and gone through all these tests and examinations, only to realize that there was no way USC was going to allow me, a Jew, to be admitted into their dentistry program.

So I stormed right out of the building at USC, walked down Jefferson Boulevard to the Southern California College of Optometry and applied that very day.

This college was not connected or related to USC, even though the names were similar. It was an entirely different organization. And I have to say that they treated me much better than USC ever did.

I didn't even really know what optometry was at the time. I had never worn glasses—I had never had an eye exam in my entire life. But I had a friend from UCLA who had said he was going there to become an optometrist after he graduated. He was a very intelligent guy, an excellent student. So I said to myself, "Well, this is a smart guy, and if he wants to be an optometrist, maybe I do too. What can I lose?" I walked in, took an application and filled it out.

My brilliant UCLA friend wound up getting his girlfriend pregnant and had to take a job to make ends meet before he ever made it to graduate school. Instead of becoming an optometrist, he wound up becoming a salesman. I was admitted to the optometry school three weeks later. Forgive me for this terrifying pun, but I've never looked back from that decision. I graduated, became a Professor of Optometry at the same school, ran my own optometry practice for 56 years, and was still working as a Staff Optometrist within the Kaiser Permanente Health system until 2014.

Back in Germany during the war, the Nazis always made a point of taking away the eyeglasses of their concentration-camp prisoners, so they would be more helpless and less likely to rebel or escape.

So it's always seemed a little ironic that I would spend my life as an optometrist, helping thousands and thousands of people to make their lives a little bit better. To help them see their loved ones, play sports, learn from books, see great works of art, experience inspiring movies and wonderful theater performances, as well as the natural wonders of the amazing planet we live on.

In our spare time, my wife Susan and I like to travel as much as we can. One of our favorite destinations is Las Vegas. I like to gamble a little: some poker, a slot machine now and then. After the life I have led—where I started, what my family and I went through, and where I wound up—I am amazed I am still able to enjoy myself every day, that I can still wake up and experience the joy of life after all these years. I can't help but feel that I'm just a little bit lucky.

Chapter 58

Return to Germany.

When I left Germany on the train to France in 1945 I vowed to never set foot on German soil as long as I lived. I kept that vow almost 70 years. There was one brief moment when, on a flight to another country in Europe, I was forced to do a short layover in the Frankfurt, Germany airport. I joked with my family and friends that I tried to float above the floor by walking on my toes while I waited for the connecting flight to take me back out of the country.

Then, a few years ago, my wife Susan's cousin was looking at a map of Cologne, Germany—my birthplace and home town—on his computer. He was using a web app called OpenStreetMap, kind of a cross between Google Maps and Wikipedia, which can show information that people contribute superimposed on a searchable map of the planet. He called me over to look at a bunch of orange dots scattered over the city. We found that they were the locations of small brass-covered stones called *"Stolpersteine,"* or stumbling blocks, that had been embedded into the sidewalks.

A Cologne artist named Gunter Demnig had created an ongoing project designed to remind Germans of what they had done—and to memorialize the innocent victims of the Holocaust—by embedding brass-covered stones in front of the last residence from which each victim was taken. The original idea of the "stumbling stones" was taken from an ancient, antisemitic German custom of saying "There must be a Jew buried here," whenever they tripped over a protruding cobblestone. It's a bigoted, backhanded way of saying: "If it's annoying, a Jew must be the cause."

By setting these stones so they stick up from the surrounding sidewalk—so you are actually likely to stumble over them—Demnig turned this custom on its head. He turned it from a rude saying into a daily reminder of Germany's guilt and responsibility—a persistent, permanent tribute to what the German people did to the Jews and other persecuted minorities.

Photo: NSDOK Museum, City of Cologne

*The Stolpersteine memorial "stumbling blocks" of
Hans Isidor Oster and Elisabeth Haas Oster, Henry Oster's parents,
at 15 Blumenthalstrasse, Cologne, Germany.*

We found out that my parents had been memorialized by *Stolpersteine* in front of the our last apartment in Cologne, at 15 Blumenthalstrasse.

Discovering that somebody—a German, no less—had gone out of his way to create memorials for my mother and father was a profound and disturbing experience. It brought it all flooding back to me. My memories of my family, my home, my relatives, and all the horrors we had been through poured over me like a breaking wave at Sunset Beach.

I felt very grateful to the artist, Gunter Demnig, and to the people at the Cologne museum who had helped him uncover and document the stories of all the victims—Jewish or not—who were ripped from their homes and murdered.

I had a couple of suggestions, though—a fact that will not surprise my friend and co-author Dexter or my wife Susan. The stones for my parents were placed in front of the apartment house we had been forced into after the Nazis had taken over. I didn't think of this place as my home. Rather, it felt more like the first prison we had been forced into, at the beginning of all the madness. If it had been up to me, I would have wanted my parents' memorial to be placed in front of our real home, at 12 Brabanterstrasse, instead.

I also noticed that the facts on my mother's stone weren't quite correct. It says that she was murdered along with my father, in Lodz. Which was all anybody—anybody except me, of course—knew about what had happened to her. My father's death was a part of the Lodz Ghetto hospital records, but the Germans kept no records when they dragged her and me from Lodz to Auschwitz. And they certainly never left a record of what happened to her that first night at Birkenau—as far as the rest of humanity knew, it was as if she had been carried away by the wind.

I sent an email to the museum, the National Socialist Documentation Center of the City of Cologne, or NSDOK, to try to correct the record of what had happened to my parents and me. Which felt pretty strange: trying to contact Germans about what Germany had done to my family.

I got a phone call from Dr. Karola Fings, a wonderful researcher, author and historian who has devoted her career to uncovering exactly what happened during those dark years, and to educating Germans and the rest of the world. I began to understand that the Germany I had known—the Germany that caused so much death, horror and devastation—was not the Germany of today.

Dr. Fings was very interested in my story. My own recollections of my experiences in the Holocaust, and my knowledge of what had happened to my parents and myself, were important to her ongoing research. It tied up many loose ends for her and I was more than glad to share what I could to help her in her efforts to document and understand what had gone on in Cologne and what had happened to all those 2,011 Jews.

We became friends—or at least as close as is possible over the phone, and by email. I admired her for her dedication to my family's story, a story I had come to think was my story alone. As it turned out, at the time there were only two living survivors of the 2,011 Jews who were taken from Cologne to Lodz.

At one point in our correspondence, Karola mentioned that the NSDOK museum and the City of Cologne were holding an event in the summer and fall of 2011—the 70th anniversary of the deportations from Cologne to Lodz.

She wanted me to travel to Germany, to Cologne, for the event. She said she could even arrange for the City of Cologne to invite Susan and me and to pay for our travel expenses. She thought it would be important and meaningful to have one of the two actual survivors of the transports from Cologne, and of the Lodz ghetto, there to bear witness to what had happened, and to help honor the memories of all those who never lived to tell the world about what they had endured. Of the 2,011 Jews taken from Cologne by the Nazis, only 23 survived the war, she told me. And of those 23, after all these years have passed, I was the only one who could be there at the commemoration.

Dr. Fings' work, and the work of all her colleagues, is predicated on one simple principle: that the only way for humanity to prevent a horror like the Holocaust from ever happening again is to force ourselves to look, with unblinking eyes, at exactly what happened, and to understand how the unthinkable, the unimaginable, ever came to pass. If we look away, if we as a species allow ourselves to take the easy way out, to let ourselves forget and let the lessons of the past fade away, we are doomed to repeat them.

The idea of going back to Germany terrified me. It just seemed like a very terrible proposition; going back, with my teeth clenched, to the country that had labeled me a virus and which had been dedicated to my extermination.

But in the spirit of telling my story—which I have been doing, once a month at the Museum of Tolerance in Los Angeles, since 1977—I finally decided to go.

It was a moving, emotional, life-changing experience. Dr. Fings laid out the red carpet for Susan, her sister, her brother-in-law and me. She guided us all over Cologne, and even took us to see my parents' *Stolpersteine*, in front of our old apartment at 15 Blumenthalstrasse.

Neither my mother or my father has a gravestone, of course. Like millions of their fellow Jews, they simply vanished from the face of the earth at the hands of the Nazis. But now I felt that I had a place to go to feel their spirits, and to be with them.

I'm sure they would be comforted by the knowledge that even though they—and almost all of our family—didn't survive the murder and the horror, their son made it through. And knowing that their tormentors, for all their depraved and evil efforts, are now almost all dead and gone. But here I am, standing here with them, still alive and still honoring their memory.

We knocked on the door of our old apartment. An elderly woman peered out between the curtains, but she refused to come to the door. She was probably just too fearful and unsure of who we were and what we wanted to allow us into her life, if only for a few moments.

But the couple on the next floor up heard us, opened their door and invited us in. They welcomed us into their home, which was a carbon copy of our old one downstairs. They listened to our story, and were amazed to discover this ancient, brutal history of their apartment house, their street, their city and their people. They couldn't have been nicer.

As a part of the 70th-anniversary event, I was asked to speak at the official reception by Jürgen Roters, the Lord Mayor of Cologne, to a roomful of invited guests including the Consul General of the United States, many foreign diplomats and some of Karola's colleagues from the NSDOK museum.

Here's what I said, translated to English from my quaint, 1930's-vintage German.

"Honored Lord Mayor Roters and Invited Guests:

First, please forgive me for speaking in my old-fashioned German. It is the first time I have spoken it in almost 70 years, and this is the first time I have ever given a speech in my native language. I had vowed in 1945—for reasons you can probably understand—to never set foot on German soil again. Until this visit, I have kept that vow.

I am now breaking that vow. I am not making this journey out of mere curiosity. I am not here for a vacation. I am certainly not here for my own pleasure.

I am here to honor my parents and my 16 other family members who were "resettled"—that is, taken away to die—in 1941. I am here to honor the 2,011 Jews of Cologne, of whom I am one of just two survivors, who in 1941 were sent from this place to the death, the disease and the starvation of the Litzmannstadt/Lodz Ghetto.

After Lodz I survived Birkenau, Auschwitz and Buchenwald. My presence here today proves to the world that even now, after 70 long years, the total elimination of Jews from Cologne was not successful. The people who kidnapped and murdered my friends and family— nearly everybody I had ever known—are gone. But I am still here, speaking to you today.

When these horrible events took place, the world failed to understand how a seemingly civilized and cultured people could allow themselves to be so willingly and tragically misled. We try very hard, but we still fail to understand this today. And we can be sure that we will fail to understand it in the eternal future. We will never understand it. All we can be sure of is that we cannot forgive, and must never forget.

I chose to return to Cologne after these 70 years to assure the present generation of Germany that they need not carry the burden of guilt and shame of a generation past. The sins of the fathers, though unforgivable and incomprehensible to us today, should not be visited on their sons and their daughters.

Hate only begets hate. Tolerance should be the goal of the future, of all the human race. Tolerance should be the goal of the aggressors of the past. It should also be the goal of their victims.

In the name of my wife, my family and the other Litzmannstadt-Lodz survivors here with us today, I thank you Lord Mayor and the City of Cologne for your kind invitation and hospitality."

Epilogue

After graduating from UCLA in 1954, Henry Oster completed his optometry education with Bachelor of Science and Doctor of Optometry degrees from the Southern California College of Optometry in 1957. He stayed to teach as an Associate Professor at the College from 1957 to 1983.

He served as a Staff Member at the Los Angeles Cedars-Sinai Medical Center Department of Optometry for 50 years, from 1957 to 2007, and was the Chief of the Department from 1989 to 2004.

At the age of 75, in 2004, he joined the Kaiser Permanente Medical Foundation as a Staff Optometrist, serving until his retirement in 2014.

He also operated his own private optometry practice in Beverly Hills, California for 56 years, from 1957 until 2013.

Dr. Oster was admitted as a Fellow of the American Academy of Optometry in 1971. He received the Vision Service Plan Western US "People First" award for his decades of volunteer work providing optometric services to people who could not otherwise afford them.

He has been honored as a Life Member of the American Optometric Association and the California Optometric Association.

Starting in 1977, Dr. Oster has spoken once a month about his experiences as a Holocaust survivor at the Museum of Tolerance/Simon Wiesenthal Center in Los Angeles, California.

He lives in Woodland Hills, California with his wife, Susan Oster. He has four stepchildren: daughters Lisa and Harriet, and sons David and Andrew. As well as six grandchildren.

Now retired at the age of 86, Dr. Oster finally has time to do his favorite thing in the world: what he calls "Cruisin' with Susan". He and Ivar Segalowitz, who also came to the United States after the war, were still close friends when Ivar passed away in 2014.

Henry Oster is the last living survivor of the 2,011 Jews who were rounded up by the Nazis and forcibly deported from Cologne in the fall of 1941.

Acknowledgments:

Thanks to Judith Cohen, Michael Levy and Caroline Waddell of the United States Holocaust Memorial Museum Photo Archives Reference Collection for the generous help and invaluable images they provided. To Dr. Karola Fings, of the National Socialist Documentation Center of Cologne (NSDOK), Germany, for her research on the deportation of Jews from Cologne and her support of our research for this book. To my brother David Kent Ford, who provided a sharp red editing pencil, and who insists that "German Shepherd" should be spelled "German shepherd," even though that would mean a German person who manages sheep. To Henry's lovely English-born wife, Susan Oster, another fierce editor and grammarian, who hasn't realized that in America we spell "realize" with a "z". To Mike Gullickson, a fellow writer who helped us wiggle through the maze of independent publishing. And to my wife Kathy Jane Ford and our kids Brian Carolus, Christina Carolus and Tiffany Jane (TJ) Ford, who supported me and endured years of my emerging from my office at the end of each writing day growling like a teary, cranky bear, after spending another emotional day living in Lodz or Auschwitz or Buchenwald with young Henry. And of course to the force of nature known as Henry Oster, one of the most inspiring humans I have ever known.

Dexter Ford
Manhattan Beach, California
May 30, 2014

CPSIA information can be obtained
at www.ICGtesting.com
Printed in the USA
LVHW101511290922
729604LV00016B/419/J